The Jews of Hungary
and Other Hungarians

The Jews of Hungary
and Other Hungarians

The Diary of László Waldapfel
1933–1941

Translated from the Hungarian original by Frank Vajda
Edited and explanatory notes by Imre Trencsényi

2021

Originally published in Hungarian as
*Magyar zsidóság – egyéb magyarság.
Waldapfel László naplója 1933. XII. 21 –*
by Új Helikon Bt, Budapest, 2019.
1204 Budapest, Tátra tér 5–8.
ISBN 978-615-80734-7-9

The English version was co-edited
by Balázs Trencsényi

English language consultants:
Nick Tomalin and Katalin Trencsényi

Cover design:
Katalin Vasali

Book design:
Adam Pócs

ISBN 978-3-949607-00-4
e-ISBN 978-3-949607-01-1

Contents

and the dark mute cavalcade of the dead
flew by,
when suddenly, a shadow fell upon the walls
of our house.
There was silence, and the morning stopped
dead in its tracks,
it was ten,
and fluttering in the streets, was a kind of
peace and a touch of horror.

("Peace, horror" by Miklós Radnóti*)

* Miklós Radnóti, *The Complete Poetry in Hungarian and English,* translated by Gábor Barabás (Jefferson, NC: McFarland & Co, 2014).

Foreword by the Publisher of the Hungarian Edition

We wish to commend a diary to the attention of the reader, a diary, which was not meant to be presented originally to the wider public. Its author is a young man, who at the age of twenty is writing about the events in his life in the 1930s, in a school notebook. Did he ever imagine that he was writing a veritable historical chronicle? We shall never be able to find this out, because soon after the last diary entry he is called up to forced labor service. The last message from the military authorities reports that he "died" on 21 December 1942, in an area of military activity. (According to our current knowledge, this official communication could also imply death by freezing or being starved to death.)

László Waldapfel was born in 1911, and studied at Budapest University to become a gymnasium teacher like his father. The discriminatory laws of the era forbade him—as they did his siblings—to occupy a teachers' rostrum. He was also regarded as a talented mathematician. The Mathematics Research Institute in Budapest commemorates his name with a plaque amongst the names of notable Hungarian mathematicians, and likewise, a memorial strip of the Loránd Eötvös University Budapest—extending along the whole length of the walls of the Trefort Garden—preserves the memory of the former student.

What is the era that László Waldapfel lived in? The First World War, military defeat, the democratic and communist revolutions, their fall, and the consequences of the Trianon peace treaty produced a crisis in society and in the field of learning. There is a library-sized volume of literature available on this topic. Various segments of society tried to cope in various ways with this debacle. Scapegoating was not present solely during the so-called White Terror in 1919–20, but also in the anti-Semitism of the interwar regime led by Miklós Horthy, which targeted the exceptionally integrated, overwhelmingly assimiliationist Jewry, and proposed also discriminatory legislation.

Looking for a way out of this social, political, and spiritual crisis did not leave the Christian Churches untouched. The clerical groupings in service of the conservative "counter-revolutionary" regime gradually became more powerful, whilst the persons and institutions who had a more liberal or left-wing orientation were sidelined, together with those assisting the underprivileged and trying to lift them from poverty. At the same time, various reform initiatives and movements emerged, challenging what they saw as a "petrified" societal order.

Critical of the "feudal" socio-economic situation of the country, agrarian populism found numerous socially committed manifestations. Those probing the miserable status of the peasantry demanded the enforcement of social justice. In the context of the marginalization of the socialist left, the young generation of intelligentsia was especially influenced by these endeavours. At the same time, the growing social tensions, especially after the 1929 Great Depression, which undermined the fragile conservative consolidation of the mid-1920s, opened the gates for extreme-right radicalism coupled with violent anti-Semitism. In this situation members and representatives of the variegated Jewish community looked for solutions to counter the threats against them and respond to the social and cultural crisis. Assimilation increased, and it could even entail an orientation toward Christianity and its formal acceptance or opting for an internationalist socialist radicalism. Other groups entertained ideas of cultural and social dissimilation, reframing their Jewish identity, which might also involve emigration or mounting a political and cultural resistance inspired by Zionist ideas.

A rude reply to all these attempts at orientation, the dramatic geopolitical and ideological changes caused by the advance of totalitarianism promptly reached Hungary in the second half of the 1930s. Hitlerism overwhelmed Germany, and soon after conquered a significant portion of Europe. Armed conflicts began, local tensions escalated into the most immense war in world history, and the legalized discrimination of the Jewish populations eventually culminated in the "Final Solution" and the gas chambers. As the war dragged on, the fierce battles gradually approached the borders of Hungary and its capital. In many people the fear of annihilation took hold, so sharply delineated by the great Hungarian Jewish poet Miklós Radnóti: "March On, Condemned!"

The diary of László Waldapfel immortalizes the first steps of this "walk." We commend it to the attention of our readers—with the poetical words of Radnóti—so that you

*"always know what you must do
to make it different."**

László Trencsényi

---

* Miklós Radnóti, "He Could no Longer Bear," in Miklós Radnóti, *The Complete Poetry in Hungarian and English*, translated by Gábor Barabás (Jefferson, NC: McFarland & Co, 2014).

Introduction by the Editor

When our grandchildren were given the task in school of drawing their family tree, and thus, on their level, undertaking research into their family history, we dug out for them several photos and letters hiding at the bottom of various drawers and cupboards. While browsing among these materials, we found a real treasure.

The title of the diary, written into a school exercise book by our uncle, murdered at the age of 31 on the Eastern Front of the Second World War because of his ethnic origins, promises a private chronicle of the events of the 1930s, but offers much more. It contains the reflections of a sensitive soul transitioning from his student years towards adulthood, but never quite arriving there due to his tragic death. It contains reflections about macro-historical events, the erupting wars culminating in genocide, but also on the more subtle internal developments and the characteristic cultural and intellectual challenges of the period.

It is thus not a typical adolescent diary. Born in 1911, he already has a complex cultural and educational background which would normally offer him a splendid scholarly career. His father, János Waldapfel was a prominent pedagogue with reformist ideas, representative of the fin-de-siècle generation of upwardly-mobile Central European Jewish intellectuals who were committed to an agenda of modernization, developing strong patriotic sentiment, while also preserving their attachment to reform Judaism. László's older siblings also started scholarly careers in the 1930s, even though the increasing racial discrimination made it impossible for them to get proper academic positions before 1945. After the war, in a very different situation, becoming adherents of the communist regime which seemed to offer an internationalist solution to the problem of racial discrimination, his two brothers and sister all became prominent scholars: József in the field of literary history, Eszter in archival studies, and Imre in classical philology. The oldest brother, Gábor, however, chose a different path, becoming a high-ranking clerk in the economic "empire" of the Weiss Manfréd company, the biggest industrial conglomerate in the country at the time, which (as we will see later) most probably contributed to his arrest and untimely death following the German occupation of Hungary in March 1944.

There is little written about the father figure in the diary, but if one goes deeper into the history of the family, we will see that he played an important role in the life of his children as well as in the orientation of his youngest son.

János Waldapfel was born one year before the Austro-Hungarian compromise, and the determining decades of his youth overlapped with the promising economic and cultural modernization of Hungary. In this period, the previous barriers to the social advancement of Jewish burghers, entrepreneurs, and intellectuals were lifted (all this was symbolically linked to the introduction of civil marriage in 1894) and although anti-Semitic discourse was present (and was even reinforced in the 1880s), it could be considered a leftover from the past which would be gradually eliminated by the unstoppable march of modernization.

Nevertheless, this period was also marked by serious contradictions. In the dual Monarchy the Hungarian political elite still felt insecure both in view of the central power in Vienna and the emerging national movements of the non-Magyar population in the country. In order to meet these challenges, the Hungarian political class was trying to speed up the process of assimilation of the nationalities, suppressing their educational institutions and trying to extend the use of Hungarian in the public sphere.

János Waldapfel grew up in the multiethnic region of Upper Hungary (today Slovakia), populated by Slovaks, Hungarians, Jews, and Germans. His father was a Jewish innkeeper with Hungarian identity but no knowledge of the Hungarian language, coming from a village with mostly Slovak peasant population but also a sizable Jewish community. János' background and his early socialization in the area of Trenčín (Hun. Trencsén) made him aware of the complexities of his patria, and after his move to Budapest (and his study trip to the University of Jena, a contemporary center of reform pedagogy) he remained emotionally attached to his native region. Along with the mainstream liberal discourse of the time, most prominently expressed by the political theorist József Eötvös, he argued in many of his writings that the minority populations could retain their mother tongue in the private sphere and also their popular culture, but at the same time with the help of adult educational societies should learn Hungarian language and culture that could also help them to enjoy the fruits of political and socio-economic modernization, thus becoming patriots of a politically unified but ethnically and culturally still pluralistic Hungary.

This was a beautiful liberal vision, but it was increasingly becoming obsolete as the Zeitgeist moved toward a more intransigent—Social Darwinistic—version of nationalism, projecting an implacable struggle for survival among the different nations, undermining the conception of multiethnic political nationhood. This became obvious, during the World War (if not earlier), and the concomitant collapse of the Habsburg Monarchy in 1918.

With the dramatic demise of the world of the belle époque he grew up in, János Waldapfel's career also suffered a setback after 1919 when the anti-Semitic new regime considered him unreliable and marginalized him even though he could hardly be expected to have any sympathy toward socialist radicalism. He continued his reformist pedagogical work until his early retirement in 1924. This is relevant here mainly from the perspective of comparing the life-worlds and ways of thinking of the father and his children's generation. It can be described as two rather divergent stories of acculturation and assimilation. The differences are not due to intellectual factors (we can see rather a strong continuity here) but the divergence of the historical contexts. The liberal self-confidence rooted in an impressive professional career and remarkable social network of the father contrasts vividly with the social and institutional marginalization and identity crisis of the son, who could not even start his academic career. With his teacher's diploma, he could not find a permanent job and could be happy that with the help of his brother he was eventually hired as a clerk in the cannery owned by the Weiss family.

He did not dream of such a life! While studying mathematics and physics at the university, he was also interested in pedagogical, psychological, and philosophical questions and was busy attending seminars on these topics at the university and intellectual circles outside of it. From the short references in the diary, it becomes clear that his circle of friends consisted mainly of those who attended these seminars and debate circles.

While the references to daily events and these institutions and networks must have been self-evident 85 years ago, today the editor of this diary needed to do thorough research to decode them. When reflecting on these names and organizations, it becomes evident that one of the most interesting aspects of this diary is the network of connections that could form around a Hungarian student with Jewish background in the intellectual universe of the mid-1930s. It is all the more surprising that we find out that most of the knots of this network were made from the very same thread, namely the Protestant "Awakening movement" born in Northern Europe and having strong repercussions in Hungary as well. The reader can find a more detailed description of this movement in the notes of the volume.

As for the Jewishness of László and the complex story of assimilation and dissimilation reflected in his diary, two important clarifications are due. At the very first "proper" entry (not accidentally, 24 December 1933) he reflects on his resolution to study the Bible (both the New and Old Testaments): "it is about time that I know what it means that I am a Jew,—not only in the general terms I am aware of at present." From the entry we can also find out that László was tempted by the idea of leaving behind his inherited Jewish religious tradition and joining a community seeking to face the social problems of Hungary in the spirit of the Gospels.

However, in the historical storm the idea of conversion was dropped as it became clear to him that being or not being Jewish was not the matter of a philosophical or theological choice of values. As the anti-Semitic legislation was unfolding from 1938 and the atmosphere became increasingly suffocating, László started to think of emigration but he did not feel comfortable in the Zionist milieu organizing this. In his entry from 6 October 1938, six months after the first anti-Jewish law limiting the economic and cultural presence of Jews, he reflected on a Zionist meeting discussing emigration and expressed his distance both from Hungarian and Jewish "nationalism," while stating that "the situation in internal politics created a huge divide between the Hungarian Jews and the other Hungarians."

When we recommend this book to the attention of a readership beyond Hungary, we hope that most of the text speaks for itself. A smaller part, due to the historical distance from the events and contexts depicted, however, needs explanation. We hoped to revive all the words (events, persons, and organizations) of this diary, covered by the debris of decades that passed between the 1930s and today. In some cases, this was easy to do, relying on readily available secondary sources and references, but in other cases we had to proceed from source to source, hint by hint, to find a solution. This was the most interesting "detective work"—but there were also some riddles (though not too many) which proved irresolvable. We hope, however, that they do not prevent the reader from understanding the essence of the "story."

Imre Trencsényi

"Perhaps taken in peacetime…"

The second person from the left is László Waldapfel, at a place not known, and with persons unknown.

The Diary of
László Waldapfel

21 December 1933–

1933.

1933. december 21.

A mai bejegyzésem inkább csak előszó a naplómhoz, mintsem tulajdonképeni naplóbejegyzés. Ma nincs valami különösebb írni valóm. De már napok, vagy hetek óta gondolok rá, hogy megint kezdjek naplót írni. Célszerű ma kezdenem és az előszót nem akkor írni, amikor az események zúgását, örömeim szárnyalását, vagy bús repesését, hangulatom kellemes, langyos lehelletét, frissítő habját, vagy indulatok vad hullámzását kell festenem.

Mért írok naplót? Érdemes-e, miért érdemes naplót írni? Minden esetre valamennyire ok magában az is, hogy eszembe jutott, hogy írjak.

1933

Today's entry in my diary is more of a foreword rather than a proper entry. Today I have nothing special to write about. But for some days and weeks now I have been thinking about writing a diary again. It is logical that I ought to start writing today and write the foreword not at that time when the march of events, the flight of my emotions, their sad downturn, or the pleasant, soft, warm breath of my feelings, their refreshing waves or the wild fluctuations of my angry disposition must be depicted.

Why write a diary? Is it worth writing a diary, and why is it worthwhile? In any case at least it is a reason in itself that it came into my mind to write one at all. There is no reason to talk myself out of it. One reason for the intention to write a diary is psychological, namely that I want to write one. Nowadays I busy myself with the problems of the nature and types of human endeavours; this is only at its inception, perhaps it will develop into something tangible. My writing a diary is a phenomenon along these lines of thought. For some reason, the thought arose, or let us say a desire to do it. I think that it will provide a permanent opportunity for producing something, which I wish to achieve. As far as the diary is concerned, it may become a product, a result which is not without interest. I shall create a memento for myself, which I shall be pleased to read later on. There may be events occurring around me which will be interesting, and which will be at least worthy of me reading about them later, and may be interesting for others as well. It is not without significance that the diary may give a more or less faithful picture of a soul: my own soul. A description of my development with its numerous conclusions may be used to arrange my life and perhaps be used as psychological material. Not only by me, but by others as well. I think it would be reasonable if everybody or many more people wrote diaries. I feel that they could become an important source for the study of psychology. Beyond these considerations, another of my aims is the intention to communicate my trains of thought thereby. Those trains of thoughts and feelings, which have not been crystallized into poetry, short stories, tales, nor have been appropriately based on evidence, nor become structured around science, or philosophy. In any case it would be a great loss for the literature of diaries if everybody ruminated so much on whether they ought to write a diary, especially if the result is negative. So perhaps it is useful; the result is an essay about writing a diary. A sort of foreword. If I wished to grandstand even more, I would write the date under the title, not above it, as I will do with further annotations. I would also sign it as "The author." But I will not do this.

See you again, Mr Diary!

Today I started reading the Bible. I found this a desirable thing to do from many points of view. Partly, because so many people regard the Bible as a book of guidance (although these days this comment applies more to the New Testament than to the Old Testament), and I wish to try to solve my problems from this perspective as well. On the other hand, our culture is so impregnated with the Bible that in order to understand fully numerous pieces of writings, many social and political movements, and certain souls, it seems essential to have a knowledge of the Bible (the Old Testament). All the above point to the fact that we are facing a classical work, which appears worthwhile to get to know. Finally, and not the least importantly, I must consider that it is about time that I know what it means that I am a Jew—not only in general terms I am aware of at present. One of the steps to understand this is a familiarization with the Bible (the Old Testament). As a matter of fact, if I wish to reproduce the way the plan arose, the starting point, as I recall, was the New Testament. When I was listening to a series of lectures by István Benkő[1] entitled "Christ," organized by the Pro Christo Student Association of Budapest[2], it occurred to me that I ought to get acquainted with Christianity by reaching to its most important and most legitimate source, namely the four Gospels. On the other hand, it is not proper that I ought to neglect my own (which in view of my relationship to a minority is my own, even though the majority also regard it as theirs in a certain sense), without ever knowing it, and so turn to another in such a one-sided manner. On the other hand, to judge the New Testament fairly, the Old Testament is indispensable. This does not mean that I must wait to finish the Old Testament before reading the New Testament. But, somehow, I earn the right to read the New Testament if I possess a certain goodwill to understand the Old Testament. If I learnt more about it and understood the Jewish religion, then I have more justification for leaving it or I may gain deeper motivations to stand by it than the motivations which have hereto existed. I do not at present vow even to the latter possibility, do not swear to heaven and earth that I shall never leave it. I am not merely a moral person. Almost certainly, I do make and will make further concessions. Also there exist other forces which weaken one's will, or even destroy it in a certain sense. For the moment, the question arises that a knowledge of the Bible is a requirement for the cultural education of a person and certainly of my cultural education, and it is not to be neglected. We must not forget that from the viewpoint of philosophy and psychology, the concept of religiosity, and the collective phenomena and ideas related to it are based on this most important document: the Bible.

Having re-read the above details, it occurred to me that the details about leaving Jewishness may create the impression of a person lying to himself, or hesitant, or (I

cannot even describe accurately) of a person not to be
held in high regard by public opinion. But I decided that
even if this were the case, it is to be included here, because it belongs to the character of such a person, and—
although it sounds paradoxical—I feel that truthfulness
requires that these lines be retained in the diary.

30 December 1933

Today, at last—after days of preparation—I went to see
Selényi[3] in order to ask him if I could go regularly to the
laboratories of the Tungsram Works where he is employed, to get some practice. For the time being we are
talking only of a month until February 1st, until I start
my practice at school. Selényi was not encouraging, but
he promised to try everything, and he would let me
know about the result in writing. It would be very good
to have some regular employment and a little activity,
even some productivity (even if not in the highest sense
of the word), not mentioning what I could learn there,
which I believe could become very valuable.

31 December 1933

Today I went to the cinema to see a film entitled
"Forbidden." I have been planning to see it for weeks, it
was shown infrequently, at least since the time I had decided to see it, but I always missed it. Hédi Victor[4] spoke
about it in the sense that the film was depressing, at least

for her, but she said it may not be depressing for me. That is the reason I wished to see it. (This is a case in point relevant to the examination of wish, desire, ambition, and curiosity.) I imagined it would be a factor in getting to know Hédi, and furthermore there exists in me—and I do not consider this to be a peculiar individual trait—a certain tendency to do things jointly together, to get on the same wavelength with her, to get involved with things that matter to her, as though living with her, to unite with her a little, besides preserving our duality. I can thank my friendship with Hédi for many warm, fine experiences, even if not all were joyful. Of course, her feelings towards me are likely to be different and probably more feeble, and this does disturb somewhat the above mentioned feeling of joining together.

As far as the film is concerned, I cannot truly say it was beautiful. Its brief content is that a married man gets to know a girl in the course of travelling, and only later when they develop a strong bond of love, he admits to the girl that he has a wife. The girl breaks off the relationship, and later has a child. They cannot break apart and the man again disturbs the girl's tranquillity. The film ends with the girl, on account of a letter she had received, shooting and killing a journalist whom she had married. Her lover becomes Governor. We witness his death, with the girl also present. She inherits the wealth of the Governor. I do not quite understand why it is necessary to make films like that, but the actors play well, there are some very powerful scenes, strong reality, undeniably. This reality contributes to make some people depressed, especially if they are already feeling unhappy, even before the film. I am not certain what specific reason could have made Hédi depressed, and why she assumed that it would not depress me. Maybe she did not mean it this way, merely to indicate that I do not empathize with literary heroes, at least in her opinion. The cinema showed a score of other films. One of them was very amusing: entitled "You Said a Mouthful."

1934

Today I performed some psychological experiments amongst the boy scout cubs of the Budapest Israelite Community (in relation to the similarity of visible objects). The little boy scouts were very friendly. They are kept occupied by my friend Pál Vidor[5] (who is not their permanent leader). One might criticize their rituals, but overall, they spend their scout group exercise time quite well and agreeably. After a ritual Grand Howl and the prayer "Shema Yisrael" they repeated what they had learnt on the last occasion about saluting and discipline. Some of the boys participated in this with intelligence and individual initiative. They participated on their own initiative, and cleverly interpreted and invoked certain symbols, which were not even mentioned earlier (e.g., 3 fingers representing the national colours, 2 fingers signalling the 2 Torahs—presumably meaning the two tablets of the Torah).

Afterwards they sang, followed by a Talmudic story about Alexander the Great, which was explained to them by Pál Vidor and which they reenacted again, as they had already rehearsed it at the previous meeting. Then they performed another story (about Hillel) as an improvisation. Their imagination is given a free rein, Pali directs them only occasionally with some instructions. They do everything with great enthusiasm, and good spirits, in a clever manner and as disciplined as possible. One can say disciplined, because this is what constitutes discipline. I found all types of children here. A bright-eyed, intelligent-looking, healthy boy; a puny, quietly cooperative boy; a knowledgeable, very anxious slim boy; a jolly, fat, sturdy little boy.

I had some difficulty getting my experiments understood. Not as regards the instructions, but to satisfy their curiosity, what this is all about. On the basis of the preparations, some of them expected some magic show. Pál Vidor then wished to help me and explained that it was an "observational race."

Fine, but what is the prize for the winner? One of the children asked this, exactly. I told them there were no prizes. However, I did not tell them that we do not even discuss place-getters. We ought to work out some format of a race for the purpose of these experiments or we need to humbly admit that this is not a real race and tell them the genuine purpose of the experiment. Perhaps we could make it a subject of the race that we wish to observe how consistently they perform after repeating the tests. I shall continue over several Thursdays when they have their "wolfpack" ritual.

I received a note from Selényi that he cannot oblige my request, because he is only allowed to employ inexperienced workers with permission from the managing director's office and the chances for obtaining this permission appears unlikely at this time. I should report again at the start of summer.

Today I continued the psychological experiments with the cub scouts. Afterwards I admitted to the boys that it was not a race or competition. One of the boys soon worked out that it was a test, and another boy the slim, know-all and very anxious boy, called Peti Szabolcsi, piped up with great condescension and nonchalant attitude that it was a "psychological experiment." Later on, at the same venue, I performed further experiments with the older scouts. Here my task was considerably easier. Whether their intelligence or their level of education was more advanced, or their curiosity was less, I cannot be certain. In any case they listened quietly to my brief introductory comments and in total silence and order they participated in the experiments. The resultant sheets they handed in were free of doodles, which cannot be said of the performance of a number of the younger cubs.

I have another matter to note, similarly in relation to psychology. Namely little Bálint, our housekeeper's little son who is 11 years old, told his mother (who brought him up) not to refer constantly to the revolting word "pejsli"[6] because it is ugly. (In fact, we had eaten pejsli yesterday).

Yesterday I came home in the morning. I was invited to Éva Lukács's family.

It was entertaining, but not too much. Beyond the dancing and the food and drinks, it was not very good. It was a typical "party." This does not mean either that they were pleasant or unpleasant company. I cannot use either of these appellations. It appears that I like dancing, and on those occasions, if not in the company of my own friends, dancing is the only thing I really enjoy. Besides, dancing always represents for me a problem of Weltanschauung so to speak. Namely, I am not sure that certain requirements of taste on my part (which even if not entirely theoretical, still have moral overtones) seem to be secretly in contradiction with an element of enjoyment in dancing. Perhaps we can solve this problem by saying "nil humanum a me alienum puto," extending the "humanum" to the "animale" portion. In fact, for me a rather dark sexual problem looms there in the final analysis. At the end of the party, they played two classical records on the gramophone. It was pleasant to listen to them. It cannot be said that the evening was a great event, but I cannot say that I regret that I went. Compared to my rather monotonous lifestyle, it was perhaps worthwhile to have attended this party.

30 January 1934

This evening I finished reading Kornis's epic work, "Spiritual Life."[7] It is a "great event," because I have never before read through a scientific work comprising three volumes. Also, though it may sound strange, I have never even read fully a single volume of this sort. I started some months ago, although I had the qualifying examination which interrupted me, and prevented my progress with reading. The book required a lot of patience, it was not very interesting throughout, but some portions were interesting and having read it all it was not a waste of time—I believe.

3 February 1934

I had a very pleasant encounter today. I met Ágnes Zombory.[8] I greeted her:

– I kiss your hand.

– Hello, how are you?—she said in a friendly manner and offered her hand.

– Thank you, I am fine—she then responds, happily, in passing:—I have a beautiful, wonderful child, six months old.

It was a real experience for me. What is the secret by which something like this appeals to me so much? I have no desire to debate this, no desire to make psychological, aesthetic, or philosophical comments.

Today as I was leaving the Trefort Street Secondary Training High School (where I have been working as a practicing teacher), a beggar confided in me his problems. He spoke is an unusually intelligent manner, carefully attempting to speak this way and eventually posing the question of why God does not take such a person to Himself. A person such as he only represents sadness to society, and only those who produce something ought to live (these were his words). I consoled him, by saying that conditions may improve.

He showed me his Beggar's License, which allows him only to beg by going from house to house. For this reason, two detectives took him to the police headquarters on Saturday, when two gentlemen gave him some money on the street.

I fail to understand why they permit only begging in the manner of calling at houses, and even if I understand, I think it is strange. Is it preferable to molest someone at his home, rather than in the street? After all, in the street if I wish I can ignore him, on the other hand at home I have to open the door when the bell rings. Apparently, greater energy is required from the viewpoint of the public as well as the beggars when they beg at houses. It is true, the streets are not enhanced by the presence of numerous beggars, but the other method I think is even more disagreeable, and the everyday appearance of streets is not supposed to be beautiful, anyway. I am afraid that covering up in front of foreigners is the main reason for these regulations. Is it really a utopia that there be no beggars at all? For the moment I am thinking something less brave, not that everybody should live on what money they earn, but that the issues of poverty ought to be handled by special authorities, maybe a non-denominational charity which could take over or at least support the charity work of the churches, but perhaps the latter may be able to solve the problem by themselves.

———

17 February 1934

I am in fact writing up yesterday's chronicle. Yesterday my day stretched into the current one. I visited Éva Reiländer's family, and came home only after midnight, at 1 am. Let me record some observations about the people who were there.

The behaviour of one of the boys was very interesting. Almost certainly he is used to being the centre of attention in any group in which he finds himself, or he wishes to be the central figure and feels capable of doing so. I felt he perceived me as being a rival to him, someone who ought to be beaten to death. Perhaps I discovered in the psychology of social gatherings a universal phenomenon (which ought to be a subject of further studies). If there are two central figures in a group, they beat each other. To what degree they do this to "each other," I am uncertain about, but I had discovered this trait only in the other person, and even afterwards I could not find any similar feelings or motivation in myself. I cannot however state with any certainty whether these factors operated or not as far as I was concerned.

My other observation is related to the extraordinary attitude people have towards occult things. The visitors at this party curtly and simply dismissed spiritualism outright as impossible. On the other hand, they were ready to label and accept telepathy and thought transference as not at all questionable or amazing or supernatural, and they firmly believed in these phenomena. One lady related quite miraculous stories and gave absolute credit to believing them. She spoke of a certain woman, in front of whose eyes reappeared the relatives of people who visited her, who had deceased long ago. She described them, the circumstances of their deaths, and everything appeared to add up, miraculously. She spoke also of the fulfilment of a prophecy, in such a way that at least she was able to be amazed by this. This same lady quite firmly rejected spiritualism. These viewpoints appear a little strange and paradoxical to me, but whether to attribute deeper significance to them depends on the intelligence and depth of thought of the individual concerned. I suspect that at this gathering or party these qualities did not appear to be manifest in any abundance. It may happen as well that people just chatter in order to make conversation, and the statements they make are not to be taken seriously nor can be regarded as being of any consequence.

Tonight I plan to go to the Opera, to see "The Troubadour." This is the first time in my life that I shall see and listen to an operatic performance.

Tonight I had a pleasant experience. A rather virulent argument occurred in the pedagogic Bible-group of Sándor Karácsony,[9] directed against one of the participants. Suddenly Miklós Heltai[10] jumped up and turned to one and then the other of the adversaries, in a very serious and excited manner, asking them not to argue. He was also yelling himself, but he exuded a desire to achieve tranquility. He spoke to Karácsony, who during this argument ceased to lead the group, and begged him—he used the word "beg"—to resume the leadership and let the exchange of ideas continue in the customary manner. I have observed for a long time that for this boy the concept of Christianity is not merely a phrase, what he encompasses under this aegis is a serious matter, and in fact the central thought of his life. In this field of thought, love has a major role to play.

Today I spoke up for the first time at a conference in the Training High School (Trefort). It is interesting that somehow I felt as though I was in 5th grade, speaking for the first time in the students' self-education societythis is how they had received it. They had listened with a good natured, smiling curiosity, as they would listen to a child, who is not to be taken very seriously. Am I just imagining this?

Today was my first day of teaching at the Training School, I held my first lesson overall. I substituted at first grade level for Ferenc Kármán. I did not introduce new material, just practiced what had been taught previously. I must admit, it was not easy. It is true I have not been prepared to teach and only found out at the last minute that I was to be called. A lot of time was spent on homework, finding the errors made by a boy. To explain it presented quite a difficult task for me, a mere beginner. It was difficult to instantly create examples to illustrate simple things, such as fractions and proportions.

Today I prepared myself for the lesson tomorrow. Perhaps it will go better if it takes place at all. By all means, I was delighted to have had the opportunity.

2 March 1934

Today I did not stand in for Ferenc Kármán in the 5th grade. I think that tomorrow, if he is still sick, I will deputize for him.

26 March 1934

I have read an interesting, fine, and thought-provoking little book yesterday and today. The author is Walter F. Otto, the title is *Der europäische Geist und die Weisheit des Ostens. Gedanken über das Erbe Homers*. It contains such comprehensive thoughts that it is not dependent on somebody's professional specialty to be able to read it. It opens one's eyes, it gives aesthetic information, it awakens one's interest in sculpture and poetry, which are all discussed. It makes me want to visit Athens to see the so-called Apollon-statues (so-called, because according to Otto many of them represent humans), makes me wish to read Pindar's works, which never occurred to me before. It was really worthwhile reading this small book. It is not philology, it is more than that: philosophy and much beyond that. Or perhaps philology in the highest sense of the word.

5 April 1934

Today I solved a problem (at least I think so)—which appeared in one of the latest issues of the *Jahresbericht der Deutschen Mathematiker-Vereinigung*. The task was to obtain proof that [...]*

* We decided to omit the description of this mathematical problem, owing to our lack of adequate expertise in the subject – The Editors.

The thesis is very surprising, quite wonderful, almost stunning. My proof was based on calculations of the value of Smith's determinant (Beke: Determinants), which provided the analogy. It needs to be carefully checked, to make sure I did not rejoice too early about the solution. If validated, I plan to write it up in German and send it to the Jahresbericht. Naturally, first it must be formalized in Hungarian.

6 April 1934

My solution to the problem is validated. I wrote it up and translated it. It was quite easy and brief, together with the text of the problem it amounts to no more than one and a half pages of standard sheets of paper. I may rethink perhaps one or two points of the composition, and I need to have the linguistic aspects checked as well.

9 April 1934

I had Dad read and correct the work, I copied it and sent the solution of the problem to the *Jahresbericht*.

I have not seen Hédi Victor for a long time. In fact, we used to be able to be alone and have good discussions, we spoke seriously, mostly alone, and we used to understand each other face to face. I have missed this very much. I am not certain if she has missed it too, or if she saw some problem, which she needed to dismiss, or whether she realized that I am in a bad mood or at least I cannot do anything when we meet with other people, and she sees that I miss the face to face meetings—but today she spoke about going home together tomorrow at midday (i.e. I go home and she goes to her uncle's). I relished this situation.

Today I had an unpleasant conversation with Bözsi Hirschberg,[11] although normally we have quiet and pleasant conversations with each other. We spoke about me and about others, and finally about Winkler. Bözsi and Hédi are not quite objective vis-à-vis Winkler, I think, or I am not objective, or neither of us are. It was an unpleasant discussion, I felt, for both of us.

1935

27 May 1935

This is a notable day in my life. My brother Gábor[12] is employing me for a trial period at the Weiss Manfréd Canning and Metalware company. It was very amusing to see him scrutinize my German and Hungarian language applications, which I had to embellish with two rows of figures, as a form of trial. Generally, it was amusing to have him as my boss.

I accept the whole business with mixed feelings. I cannot calculate the consequences. I do not know to what degree it would hinder my employment as a teacher or a mathematician/physicist, and I do not know, whether this field of work would appeal to me even if temporary or perhaps for a long period. It is possible that with the lapse of time I might be able to perform some work, which is related to my expertise.

For the moment it will probably be interesting, and I may be possibly able to say something to my diary, arising out of this job.

Well, then: To work!

Today was an exciting day. I think it was exciting throughout the world, where people live. So it was in our office. The Italian-Abyssinian conflict reached its culmination point. Yesterday Mussolini delivered a huge, belligerent speech, which was broadcast on radio. The public opinion here was decisively of the view that our own fate is at risk. Apart from this, Italian troops allegedly have already crossed the border to Abyssinia. In the morning we discussed the likely events that were to follow, we spoke of them also at lunchtime and periodically throughout the day. During lunchtime, I spoke with my friend Szatmári about the war. We went out to the corridor, where we met Irén Fried, Nusi Székely and Magda Kakassy. Nusi and Irén refused to listen and rejected our talk with some real revulsion, because they have had enough talk of the war in light of all discussions about it today. I said something like "we shall go and then get wounded, and you will care for us." I'd rather not nurse you—you can stay there—said Nusi. Magda, a little girl, only 15 years old, took this comment as an opportunity for a little argument and said: "If I could only see that you are no longer here." I remarked: "Child!" She is argumentative and if the war reaches her whilst still very young, she would represent, with her companions, the group of romantic enthusiasts, for whom it would be an interesting and fine holiday to see the farewell of the troops, singing (they do not know what they are doing). If there were a young man who is close to her heart and he would have to leave, she would cry while saying goodbye to him, but really seriously she would only comprehend the matter after the battle has raged for months, then she would learn what worrying means. Or perhaps she will only understand, when (and God may protect her) she becomes a widow.

I really wish for the above matters to have no consequences.

1938

I ended my last entry—more than 2 years ago— with the comment "I really wish the above matters to have no consequences." Well, the matter continued, although not quite as I have presented it. It did not affect us. The Italian-Abyssinian conflict developed into a real war, much Italian and Abyssinian blood has been shed, thus the human heart had plenty to mourn. After a long, tough battle they have conquered a nation and made the Emperor a homeless refugee. They brought civilization, which may develop into culture, to a primitive people— this is undeniable—but I cannot suppress the mood of the "Bards of Wales"[13] when I write about this. I cannot see the benefit in oppression, making a people happy by brute force, "As happy as the oxen are / Beneath the driver's yoke?" Such behavior is all the more suspect if it stems from the selfishness of a community. The war is over, and we—thank God—have not been involved.

Today is another historic day. This prompts me to take my pen to write. The referendum was scheduled to take place in Austria tomorrow, voting on—besides the basic principles of the Government—whether Austria should remain independent. Chancellor Schuschnigg was the father of this plan, and in his radio broadcast he emphasized his own personal responsibility. Tonight around 10 pm as I was coming home on the street, the newspaper boy was yelling; "Schuschnigg resigned." The street has not yet taken on an appearance worthy of this historic moment. Some people buy the paper, but there are only a few people walking in the street and thus no special mood or anxiety can develop. Whether some people who are aware of the news feel differently, I cannot comment, because I do not share their thoughts. The appearance of the street is like any other day. The event however is highly portentous, it has the odor of gunpowder, and we are fearful that it may cause major changes in the politics of many countries (amongst them Hungary as well).

The irony of fate: I read in the same newspaper that Parliament started the debate of the legal proposal involving the practically-oriented secondary schools. It is the proposal, which if it becomes law may offer the promise of a teaching post for me. Behold: the news of the spread of national socialism and at the same time another news report, which if not nullified by the consequences of the earlier news, could become a welcome development as far as my private life is concerned. Reading the paper, we can see that Schuschnigg resigned, because the German Government demanded it in an ultimatum, and it foreshadowed the entry of the Wehrmacht into Austria if the ultimatum is rejected. Schuschnigg preferred to resign. Many will judge this to be cowardice. I say that it is questionable if there exists at all a matter so important that a statesman can risk the lives of the masses of his nation. There is probably some political insight involved. He thought he may delay the decision. Perhaps Austrian independence may be solved without the sacrificing of lives. Or is perhaps the clamor for independence not entirely truthful? Is the Austrian government willing to accept the "Anschluss" in the form of an Alliance, but not as an incorporation? This appears to be the case by the constant reiteration of the German character of Austria by Schuschnigg (even in the text of the questions related to the subject of the Referendum).

We must look forward to tomorrow, with interest.

---

12 March 1938

German troops entered Austria. Hitler himself spoke on Austrian radio. Public opinion here is quite restless and anxious, and not only in Jewish circles—at least that is what I have experienced in the factory. A Polish engineer spoke thus: "A person can labor throughout his life until he secures a position, and then suddenly everything becomes insecure." This man's quiet desperation proved a quite special experience for me, indicating his fear of war per se, and fear of political turmoil.

---

1 April 1938

Today I delivered my talk about the Jewish Question at the Sociology Research Seminar, led by Brandenstein,[14] who entrusted me with the task about seven weeks ago. The assignment was very difficult. I had many doubts which surfaced during the preparations. I was thinking of resigning, but in the end, I held on. I managed to collect the material quite well, and I was able to speak in such a manner as to avoid giving any material that might feed anti-Semitism, nor to hide my own ambiguity. I tried to be objective. The public showed considerable interest. The whole duration of the evening was three hours, consisting of one and a quarter hours for the lecture and the remainder kept for discussion.

Unfortunately, overall, the debate formed in such a way that the Jewish participants defended the Jewry and the Christian discussants attacked them, but in a totally parliamentary style. The brother of Kálmán Hubay,[15] an extreme right-wing member of parliament, declared that the lecture and the debate was very interesting and that he enjoyed it very much. During the course of the debate, and including the closing remarks, which were heightened by counterarguments, both by myself as well as other Jewish speakers, Brandenstein represented the view that the question must be assessed not on moral or judgmental basis, but it must be admitted that that there is a power struggle between Jews and Hungarians. The most desirable solution to this would be if the Jews were less active and were not featured in leadership positions beyond their proportion within the population, because this would lower the reaction. He represented the viewpoint to fully accept the facts, as they exist, but with his customary brilliant mind and clear analyses. My lecture I think failed to convince those who had other opinions, but as a lecture, I feel it was more successful than I had hoped (I delivered it freely, without notes).

I was searching amongst my old writings and fragments. I looked at some of these scientific contributions with a certain melancholy. I wrote them some years ago. I can now see that they represented a high level of achievement, they were like "lion's claws." It was all just beginning, even now I start this and that, but ever more infrequently and I rarely get beyond the beginning. My older initiatives were worthy of a burgeoning talent. But it is not real talent or at least not a talent of real worth, which merely starts off something and produces only a fraction of the work. Perhaps it may serve as some excuse for me that my circumstances are not ideal for performing scientific work.

I reviewed my attempts to study the question of trust and the basis of geometry, and this contributed to my present mood...

I arrived back very tired after two days of excursion over Easter, so I only write about it today. We went to Tahi on Saturday afternoon,[16] we slept there and started climbing hills the following morning. We went to Paprét via Rókakapu, along the serpentine which presented a superb view, from there to Nagyvillám, then descended to Visegrád.

We arrived at Visegrád in the evening. We started looking for lodgings. In one of the pubs the accommodation was quite expensive, in another there were no rooms for guests, the third one had no vacancies. Finally, we were able to get accommodation—at 6 pm—in the Bischitz villa, where my brother József and his family stayed two years ago on a summer holiday. The rooms were adequate, not fantastic, but clean and overall inspired confidence.

At Visegrád we heard something of the extreme right-wing mood in the countryside. It is terrible that these days going to a village here and there one becomes reminded—without necessarily any concrete reason—that the people in the villages are enemies of Jews. From time to time a Jewish tourist gets overwhelmed by a certain unfriendly feeling.

Nature however offers compensation for this. We observed some very fine scenery along the way. From Visegrád to Dömös, along the Téry way, from Szakó pass to the Hoffman springs, to the Hoffman-shack, and from there across Malomvölgy to Pilismarót. From there we returned by boat.

We have experienced rain, snowfalls, and on Sunday beautiful sunshine. We saw many nice things. I took some photos. The whole tour was very pleasant.

Today I went to the International Trade Fair. Apart from the minor exhibits, the most interesting items were the television demonstration by Phillips and the Capability Tester by BSzKRT.[17] The television, as seen here, is not yet perfect. It produces a slightly distorted and slightly foggy image, but in any case, it has reached the stage that the human form looks like a human form, and the human face looks like a human face. Movements are quite clear, but the technique is not yet capable of providing perfect artistic pleasure. In the evening, after returning home, I made the special observation that watching something far away on television did not affect me as a major or sensational experience. It is not comparable to the experience, which I had in childhood, when I first looked down a microscope. Apparently, no technological achievement can surprise me today, nor does it give me an uplifting feeling. We have heard so much about television and in general we must feel that in the field of technology nothing is impossible, so that we by-pass similar experiences as common, everyday occurrences.

We had the oppurtunity to test our capabilities at the BSzKRT exhibit. I tried it on myself as well, and I must admit I was not very successful.

A week ago, Kálmán Hubay, a national socialist member of parliament gave a lecture at the Seminar of Social Research, entitled "What is Hungarism?" Three days later I recorded my observations in a letter, because at the site I did not feel the situation suitable to address remarks. I sent off my letter today, comprising over ten pages. I am curious how he will react to it.

According to the newspapers, the Darányi Government will resign today and Béla Imrédy[18] will form a new government. The journal Magyarország even carried the "final" list of members of the new government, although from the reports it appears that there exists a certain ambiguity about the persons of Bornemissza and Hóman. We look forward to the events with some anticipation.

The Saturday edition of *Új Magyarság* dated 21 May, carries Brandenstein's piece, in which he provides a reply to Géza Féja's article in Magyarország, entitled "Lecture by an Arrow Cross Leader at the University."

The article objects to the fact that Hubay was allowed to speak at the Seminar of Social Research. Brandenstein on the contrary declares that this does not mean the expression of one-sided opinions, because at the Seminar all kinds of worldviews may be expressed. To support this statement, he mentions my lecture about the Jewish Question.

By the way, yesterday the Upper House accepted the Jewish Law.[19] They have only forgotten to add one clause to the closure, at least as far as I remember the text. This clause is to state "that all laws contrary to this lose their validity."

It would have been necessary to add this customary formula, because two laws contrary to each other in a sense are in effect. No matter how far this question is twisted in the parliamentary debates by the Government and its parties, this law contradicts the 1867 Law of Emancipation. The debate in the upper house was of high quality, especially the speech by László Ravasz,[20] although it did not embrace philosemitism. Immanuel Löw[21] expressed the pain of the Jewish community, but also expressed his acquiescence as a law-abiding citizen. He also expressed his faith in the restoration of equality before the law. Lajos Láng, a Jewish representative also spoke intelligently, and gave open minded, serious comments.

28 May 1938

I went to the Artists' Theatre today to watch a performance of *Magyar Csupajáték* [Hungarian Fullplay] by Paulini.[22] Unusual performance, consisting of nine musical, dancing, singing portions. They dance to the tune of folk-style Hungarian music, they mime and sing. There is a lot of naiveté as well as artistry involved. One watches the performance with interest, but in certain sections the most interesting aspect is that it dares to exhibit its trivial and primitive creation set in an artistic-type performance, in a somewhat stylized manner. If we reflect on the fact that this is what makes the play interesting, it reduces its artistry in our eyes. But this does not apply to it all. Furthermore, there are no scenes that are completely worthless shown in the whole performance. To try to transform this to a general style or artistic direction would be a hopeless task, but to produce it as a single piece was of value. Paulini, as he explained in his enthusiastic speech which he delivered before the last item, attributes greater significance to the work. He predicted that it would have a great role in the formation of artistic scene of the coming years.—Perhaps the best parts were the singing item "The wood gatherer," and the "Snowman family," a singing, dancing grotesque scene. In the first one, an actress, whose name I do not know, depicts a woman who is gathering wood, whilst singing. She played brilliantly, presenting a fine song and using her voice and all her movements to splendidly characterize the wood-gathering old woman. The story behind this was also extremely naive, but that does not detract from it. In the latter scene, one of the other performers played the role of an old drunkard, dancing, singing, and making movements, he was highly amusing. One or other of the pieces served as a platform for fine dances. We also saw an interesting silhouette-picture. One of the scenes was played out entirely, almost from start to finish in the form of silhouettes. The music was at times definitely and irritatingly dissonant, hurting your ear. Even if such things exist in folk music, to transplant them to artistic music does not enrich it, in my opinion.

I listened to this performance with mixed feelings right to the end, but I cannot say at all that it was a pity to have gone to hear it.

21 September 1938

Today the air raid commander, chief engineer Riedl, held a meeting in the factory. The lecture created an anxious mood amongst us because we felt that this was not a theoretical issue, but one that affects us very closely. The lecture bore signs of rapid action to be taken. So far, we have not devoted much time to thinking seriously about air-raids, but the question arose that in the coming day this may become an actuality.

They may become an actuality, but there is no certainty that they would indeed occur. For some days now we have felt that we are living in historic times. We look for the news, will there be an outbreak of war, or not. Nobody knows for certain.

Today there was a large revisionist assembly at Heroes' Square. It has almost certainly raised the enthusiasm for war, which so far has not been shown to be very evident. The pictures with which modern war is depicted are too horrific for people to create much enthusiasm for fighting.

Today we can read in the newspapers that the Germans entered Sudetenland to maintain order, for the time being working hand in hand with the local authorities. However, the annexation of the territory and its joining Germany is a fait accompli. The whole development is for the moment unclear, but Hungary also entertains high hopes. Yesterday's great public rally also demanded quite energetically the return of Upper Hungary. [23]It is impossible to foretell at this point how the whole transition will evolve, in terms of external and internal politics.

Today's papers report that Czech soldiers again occupied those areas where the Germans, according to yesterday's reports, already started to settle in. The evening papers speak of clashes between Czech and Sudeten German forces, resulting in numerous casualties. The air smells of gunpowder.

Today a number of men of various military age categories were called up, but they are designated not as regular army groups, but rather as "volunteer Freikorps." They are not even dressed up in uniforms, and the plan is to send them to Upper Hungary and possibly have them occupy the area. The papers do not write about this. I heard the news from Tibor Szalai, who was called up.

Just to indicate that we live in such anxious times—I bought three newspapers today.

In the morning we had an air raid drill in the factory. It merely consisted of marching down to the courtyard, where the chief engineer Riedl said a few words about how to behave in case of an air raid alarm. Afterwards the sirens signaled that the air raid was over, whereupon we returned to our workplace. It barely took three minutes by the time everybody arrived from the workshops and offices to the courtyard. The whole business was carried out in perfect calm, fairly speedily, and over a few minutes. Naturally, we cannot expect that in case of trouble it would happen as smoothly, but after many drills of this kind, it may be possible to achieve a result close to this. After all, in case of danger, a normal person cannot conquer the panic entirely but maybe it will be remembered how easy it is to empty these factories completely in a short time. Therefore, there is no need to push and crowd in, as it would only increase the danger.—Let us hope it will not come to this, but we cannot be convinced that it will not occur.

---

25 September 1938

Tonight, I went to the movie. I saw the "Nightingale of Hearts," starring Deanna Durbin.[24] One of the nicest films I have ever seen. Pleasant, entertaining piece. Deanna Durbin plays enchantingly well; she sings nicely and she represents joy and kindness with her whole demeanor. This is further enhanced by the many other pretty young girls. The film takes place in a Swiss college for young women. It has excellent photography. It is nice to be able to spend two joyful hours in these stressful times.

Because reality is not very cheerful. This morning the papers reported that Hitler sent a memorandum to Prague, in which he affirms his demands. The paper tried to explain this step as an easing of tension. In the evening the *Hétfői Napló* [Monday Diary] reports that Prague does not accept Hitler's demands. This does not amount to a detailed account of the text of the reply, but information gleaned from the Czech side.

Tomorrow there will be a major air raid alarm exercise. Gabi thinks it will be quite a serious exercise, which in case of necessity may develop into a major air defense function, although it may be an exaggeration to say that this may happen, at least it is not likely. But at any event, Prague's above noted position and the many rumors, which often turn out to be true, indicate the gravity of the situation. It is alleged that we have already sustained casualties, although the war according to our knowledge has not begun. There is talk of general mobilization taking place tomorrow. We can record a joke which arose a few months ago:

– "I know a rumor.

– What is it?

– All rumors are true."

One thing is certain. Our lives are not dull.

At the time of writing, we have had two air raid exercises. One took place in the morning the other in the evening. I took no active part in either. In the morning I heard some rifle-shots and cannon shots, and, in the evening, I saw some anti-aircraft searchlights. The preparation on our part consisted of covering up three windows with black paper. The instructions were to prevent any light escaping. The air raid alarms were not overly powerful, they would not have woken up a man soundly asleep. The authorities ought to remedy this.

In the evening, partly at the time of these exercises, Hitler gave a long speech in the Sportpalast in Berlin, which was also broadcast by Radio Budapest. He described his "peace policies" and spoke of Czechoslovakia and "Herr Beneš" in a strident, contemptuous voice. Unfortunately, I could not listen to all the speech, because Aunt Ernestine, at whose flat I listened, got so anxious that she could not bear listening, and turned off the radio before the end of the broadcast. It is likely that at the end, Hitler in a more or less decisive manner expressed his determination to go to war.

Whilst I am writing these lines, the air raid siren started sounding—again fairly softly—it seems that another exercise is to begin.

I visited Imre Groszman[25] and family, with my sister Eszti.[26] The discussion was very unusual and most depressing. It revealed very sharply the currently existing opposition between the Jews of Hungary and the Hungarians' desires, feelings, and interests and Hungarian society as a whole. It is desperate that things have developed this far. It is barely tolerable that the Jews live here, tied by a thousand links to a society which accepted them, but that their existence here is not happening naturally and their ties with the original population are not really binding. I am not talking from a Hungarian nationalist perspective, after all I am only a nationalist with a lot of provisos and caveats and in any case different than others. Today I am already at a crossroads, even if I accept nationalism as such, does it make me stand alongside the Hungarians or alongside the Jewish people. As I say it is not my own nationalism which is hurt by this Jewish general attitude (although traditions influence our feelings involuntarily), but what I find painful is that Jewish people do not stand opposed to Hungarian national aspirations because their philosophical convictions lead them to internationalism (if this were the case, then probably the stance of the Jewish people would be as mixed as those any other groups—although the majority of Jews have a position similar to the one experienced at Groszman), but they oppose Hungarian national aspirations because the situation in internal politics created a huge divide between the Hungarian Jews and the other Hungarians. This conversation sharply forced upon me to face the horrible historical fact, which is the lot for the Jews and from which I cannot see an escape. I have barely spoken the whole evening, because to debate and counter the arguments in such questions is not possible. The differences in interests are so sharp that it is impossible to deny them without lying and without slapping one's ego in the face. We ought to say rather that there exists no solution, other than trying to earn the positive recognition and respect of our environment, and also to force ourselves to a mode of action which is in accord with the wishes and interests of this nation. Also, we need to feel a certain duty even to deal with those who harm us, if we decide or we are forced to stay. Or we should remove ourselves away from this country, and then we must not tolerate that the official Jewish leadership should issue pompous nationalistic statements and thus attempt, unsuccessfully, to help the situation. Perhaps the above-mentioned method in time restores the earlier intimate harmony, which could of course only be labelled harmony if the good relations are held mutually. This eternal ebb and flow are barely a promise of consolation.

13 October 1938

The negotiations are continuing in Komárom for the fifth day between Hungarian and Czech delegates on the return of the territories taken from Hungary. Today the negotiations were interrupted, because the Czech delegation put forward a proposal vis-à-vis the Hungarian demands, which is totally unacceptable. Allegedly the radio announced that Kánya declared that he sees no purpose in continuing the negotiations, and we shall turn to the Powers who are the signatories of the Munich agreement to validate our demands.

In all respects the situation is very tense. News arrives from Upper Hungary about Czech brutalities, on the other hand the Hungarian population there, intoxicated by their hopes, organize marches, protests, sing the Hungarian national anthem and people are donning Hungarian cockades. There are reports of cruel retribution by the Czechs in some places.

I am uncertain if this is the result of the external political situation or whether it was planned earlier, but we have reached a new phase in the air raid training at the factory. After official working hours we reported to the auxilary air raid shelters, where they made us sniff some gas. A few minutes after breathing it in, it had an unpleasant effect, in the form of coughing fit, lasting 10–15 minutes.

15 October 1938

Today many of my colleagues said good-bye. Those soldiers born in 1907 and 1911 had to report to their battalions. Although they are not yet to be sent to the front, as we have no war declared as yet, the farewell has serious overtones for both those departing and those left behind. I wrote "serious overtones," but this was mixed with a certain amount of bitter humor.

In the evening I attended the revisionist assembly of the Jewish youth groups and Jewish social and cultural associations. The audience filled the Goldmark Hall[27] fully. The speeches had a central theme, that we were Hungarians and at decisive moments we put aside all the harms we have suffered and fight with all our might to achieve justice for Hungary. Several times there sounded the refrain which was echoed more or less by the audience: "Return to us all the territories!" "Return Pozsony!" "Return Kassa!" "Down with Trianon!" The demonstration could be called a success…

2 November 1938

The year 1938 is a major historical year. It seems that the turbulence of world history has abated for the time being, or at least an important chapter has ended.

All that remains is a technical adjustment. In Vienna today they held the arbitrating negotiations about the Hungarian–Czech question, with Ribbentrop, the German, and Ciano, the Italian foreign minister's participation. The territories demanded by us, with the exception Újszállás and Nyitra, were returned to us. We made Pozsony [Bratislava] a subject for separate adjudication even before the decisive conference. It seems we are willing to give up our demand for it. The fate of Pozsony has not yet been decided. The occupation of the territories to be returned to us will take place from Saturday (today is Wednesday), until next Tuesday or Wednesday.

We cannot tell to what extent this result may calm the historic upheavals. We do not know in terms of internal or external politics what is likely to follow. Every new situation holds the seed of a new development. Life never stands still.

But, in any case, 2 November 1938 will be an oft-mentioned date in history.

8 November 1938

I successfully solved a mathematical problem which has occupied me for almost three years. [...] Of course, the series of problems have not yet been solved and I hope that my proof includes the possibility of making the solution universally applicable. [...] I am not sure how far I can advance but let us keep hoping.

9 December 1938

Today the first chivalrous affair in which I participated has ended. My colleague Lakatos offended my colleague Zsótér with insulting language, whereupon he challenged him to a duel. Kis Tarnay and Kriss were Zsótér's seconds, Erdős and I acted for Lakatos. We discussed the matter yesterday at midday, and today Lakatos publicly expressed his regrets. The whole affair was very amusing for me. While watching Gyurka Tarnay's deadly seriousness, the way he handled the whole thing, and the fact that such childish matters constituted the discussions and nuances that were weighed up for one and a quarter hours, I could hardly suppress my smiles, or had to grimace in order to hide my amusement.

------

20 December 1938

I had an interesting incident today. I enquired about a new brand of camera in a store. I asked "What brand is it?" The reply was made in an apologetic and resigned manner: "This is of German manufacture." In fact, I asked about it from this viewpoint, ~~because I would not like to buy German products. It is interesting that the...~~[*]

I had a pleasant conversation with Frici Docskál (now Décsi).[28] We spoke of the Jewish Question. He spoke savagely against the Arrow Cross. It was very nice of him, personally.

He made the following comment: "When I hear of these things then I usually think of Pál Erdős,[29] Tibor Grünwald,[30] and you, and if they kicked you out it would be a terrible injustice." One can only occasionally hear such warm—I emphasize: truthful—words.

[*] This is crossed out in the original handwritten manuscript.

Yesterday I attended a gathering, which is typical of our times, and seems to occur two or three times a week in an apartment in Budapest. I must describe it precisely because of its actuality. The issue in question is that some of my colleagues in the office—Jewish colleagues—have been toying with the idea of emigrating and they gather for discussions about emigration as a group. I joined the discussions yesterday and attended the first such meeting. The meeting was held at the flat of the Freisagers, who have a fine apartment in Visegrádi Street. The beautiful flat was in fact the object of an interesting observation, which is probably typical of the discussions of this sort. As soon as we had arrived, we started complimenting the apartment. Staub said "What an agreeable bekhavod[31] flat from the liberal period." "This apartment remained from the Vázsonyi Era."[32] Others were commenting that those who do not have such a nice flat at least do not suffer when they have to leave it. Lőwy said "he is happy about everything that he has not got." Before the discussion even started, they put an English Linguaphone record on the gramophone. The group meets also in order to learn to speak English. A picture of Jewish life in Budapest in 1939!...

As far as the factual part of the discussions were concerned, Salgó reported about his discussion with Baron Alfonz,[33] Director Gross, and with a lawyer. The Baron did not refuse to help but recommended that Gross ought to handle the issue. The result of discussions with Gross were that the firm will hand over the final salary entitlements to all who wish to leave, they are permitted to leave at once, and furthermore they will get a period of unpaid holiday to be re-trained. The difficulty involving currencies can be solved by the Baroness in London, who will provide the necessary sums to the group. The person of the lawyer is suspect in several respects, because he will only undertake the procurement of immigration visas if he is paid the whole honorarium in advance, and he does not accept as adequate security for the money any other form of assurance. The group refused to endorse this. They were willing to pay a portion of the fee in advance and deposit the rest elsewhere. This was acceptable for the majority. My feeling is that it is not worth starting to deal with this man.

For the moment they are talking about emigrating to Australia. We are expecting a reply from several Australian sources whether they would in principle permit the entry and settling of a group of 20–30 people. So far, we have received unfavorable replies from two sources.

Our discussions about emigration have now taken on a more concrete form. I could not decide up to this point if I ought to participate in this business. On the other hand, by tomorrow I must communicate my decision in relation to one of the solutions which has emerged. Therefore, I decided to devote today (Sunday) to think through and evaluate the theoretical and practical problems involved. I arrived at the view that I would not participate in the actual solution. However, there is another option: New Zealand. A Budapest lawyer, Dr. Widder would, as a favor, undertake the communication with an Australian lawyer who would charge only 5 pounds per head, upon arrival to New Zealand. This looks much more advantageous from several aspects, if only because it delays having to say the final word. But I shall probably participate in this plan, which does not mean that I shall make the moves to obtain the permits. Whether I shall utilize the permits (if successfully obtained) depends on the situation and the evolution of my mood.

Today I visited old Dr Lichtenstein to get the medical certificate required to obtain an immigration permit. He knew immediately that I came for a certificate and he asked me: "Well, where are you heading?" It shows that it is very fashionable to ask for certificates nowadays, with emigration in mind. In the Medical Board offices, where the medical certificate must be validated, there was another client, also looking to validate his certificate. Judging by his face probably with a similar aim in mind.

I am not resolved to emigrate as yet, but I do not wish to miss the opportunity that I do not have to arrange the matter personally and that I do not have to leave alone—perhaps for a long trip, to lead a new life. There could arise new situations, which may cause me to blame myself for missing the opportunity. Thus, I shall probably join one of the actions of the group. We are talking about New Zealand. At the end of the week or at the start of the following week we shall dispatch the documents.

<hr>

6 March 1939

<hr>

Today I was present at an interesting gathering. There was a lecture given at the Lágymányos youth group, which was entitled "Questions of Settlement." It was a very interesting lecture. At the beginning, the lecturer conveyed opinions which did not suggest that he was a Zionist, only someone who looks at the other aspects of assimilation and may represent a certain Hungarian-Jewish duality, and notes with some distress that the Hungarians do not accept our attempts to join them, as we would expect. Later on, during the course of the lecture, however, he turned out to be fully Zionist. The introduction thus appeared to be a clever trick to capture the audience. It is astonishing how strongly the propaganda techniques have been developed these days. One encounters regularly people, of whom one could imagine that they had been trained in schools for agitators. The real interest however was not the lecture, but what followed it. Under the title, "Discussion of the tourist group," "Chaver" Fenyvesi gave a fiery Zionist propaganda speech and depicted the tourist group as a hidden Betar group.[34]

He did not indicate this circumstance but took it as self-explanatory. The matter was slightly painful for the officials present and some of the youths also spoke up against mixing up the themes of the meeting. This is also characteristic of our age: these secret meetings, which can involve people inadvertently. This could be the method they used years ago to promote the Russian revolution. I must mention that Betar—according to the lecturer—operates with a governmental agreement, but it is not officially sanctioned.

1940

I just returned from Badacsony to Révfülöp.[35] It is 2 am in the morning. I must describe immediately certain thoughts that I had, the impressions which woke in me in recent times, when I kissed Kata for the first time. I wanted to write it down at that time, but technical matters interfered. These experiences developed further; I will try to describe them.

The first mystery for me is whether the actresses observe so well women driven by their emotions and produce a realistic picture or do they play-act and some women imitate them in the dark, in a romantic setting. I would like to solve this problem and find out how much of Kata's behavior is tactical and how much of it is instinctive. For me the whole experience is novel, it is possibly an everyday event for men, more experienced than myself. This is my first adventure and Kata brings a lot of illusion to play. What the aims are and what the methods are is not clear to me. Perhaps her every word is self-serving and every movement is designed in order to exploit the current mood, and the whole thing lacks tactics and technique. But it is also possible that she possesses a feminine consciousness, and that she would like to increase through me the number of hearts she has bewitched and she chooses her methods with feminine guile: such as the cleverly dropped words. Perhaps they are loaded with lies. It is said that women like to lie and they know how to do it. It is undoubtedly true that I did lie and play-act to a degree. I desired to have the adventure and I was delighted to have it. I did not fall in love with Kata, it was only an adventure for me. However, one cannot expect to have an adventure if one starts with an introduction as follows: "please, may I have an adventure with you?" I have not lied in words as such, but undoubtedly did so in my behavior. I can be excused only if Kata lies and at least she knows that I am lying. Otherwise, I would be deeply regretful and ashamed that I had lied. Today in Badacsony I play-acted the role of the lover very forcefully, as I imagine myself to behave like an actor, and use not only techniques, but true involvement. I managed to create a pleasant mood for myself as well. Kata, when I told her this plainly—amongst other overly sober remarks—commented that I would have become a good actor if I chose to do so.

In Badacsony I got quite used to the entertainment and especially enjoying myself with someone, although throughout the whole time I have been fully aware that this is just a game, it does not come from deep emotions and does not have a profound effect. Kata's sparkling eyes lent a valuable addition to the game. It is a great pity that already on the train trip home my sobriety showed a strong contrast to Kata's mood. When we got to Révfülöp, against my protests, at Magda and Bandi's request we went to the promenade and there I did not continue anything arising out of the romantic period at Badacsony. Rather than that, I made some sober remarks. It was not a fine ending to an evening. I knew what to expect and that is why I wished to go home straight away.

I was discourteously sober, unpleasantly sober and caused a disillusion. I showed my true face in its entire oddity, and its total misery. I showed that whoever is brought in close contact with me by Fate, will not do well. It is good that Kata was not brought to me in love, only in the spirit of a happy mood and for a small adventure. A happy mood, "a kiss and nothing else."[36] It is great that there are songs about this! How they help us speak!

Today the placards appeared on the streets of Budapest for the first time, carrying the slogan "Danger of Bombing!" The chief of police warns the population of the possibility of air raids and orders the "national air-raid alarm." Over the past few days, we have become aware of how very serious the political situation has become. The Yugoslav-German conflict, the suicide of Prime Minister Teleki, the combination of reasons behind it, and finally the transit of German troops southward, over the past few days (since 3 April 1941), by trucks, motorcycles, and tanks, all augured the start of the storm. This morning I went on an excursion quite calmly, in Hűvösvölgy we heard the air raid sirens, the trams stopped, but no one knew anything for certain. Somebody even told that the air raid in Zagreb would be broadcast directly, and that trams did not run as a result of a technical problem. Later we heard that that in the morning they proclaimed the air raid emergency. We boarded during another siren and the tram started to roll.

The city was almost completely dark. On the wall of our house we then could read the notice. The concierge and a few tenants sat in the dark, in the fashion we got used to during the air raid exercises. They commented that the alarm had been serious, not an exercise. The notices, which ordered readiness, spoke of the danger of bombing raids, and not of exercises. Arriving in our flat we started to darken all the windows and commenced tasting, in an expectant mood, the atmosphere of a city and life at war.

7 April 1941

There was an air raid alert in the morning. Everything turned out to be orderly and quietly organized. A much more disciplined crowd than I had dare hope. According to the news which spread at noon, Szeged, Pécs, and a few smaller Hungarian towns were bombed.

9 April 1941

I have been on guard duty in the building, between 10 pm yesterday evening, until 4 am this morning. Originally it should have been only from 10 pm to 2 am (even that is long, because in the building there are enough people to find persons for 2 hourly or even 1 hourly relief of the guards)—but the relief did not arrive, and I stayed till 4 am. The relief had not arrived even then, but I got bored and handed over my role to the concierge. I found out today that no one was rostered even after 2 am. Incredible indolence on the part of the person in charge of guard duties.

Today we had air-raid alerts twice, but there is no mention of this in the evening paper *Esti Kurir*, so I do not know what happened.

Unfortunately, two of the ladies in the factory are already showing signs of nervous collapse. There are however many who retain their good spirits and spend their time in the shelter playing "Lexicon games." The assembly in the shelters during air raids continues to take place in an orderly manner and rapidly. By the time the third siren blows (two and a half minutes) almost all people have reported to the bomb shelter.

The radio announced just now that on both occasions Yugoslav airplanes headed for Budapest, but they were forced back, before they could release their bombs.

Today, in the factory we swore the following oath; "I swear that I shall carry out the defence duties, assigned to me, faithfully, that I shall obey the commands I receive, and I shall guard any military secrets which have been entrusted to me. So help me God!"

18 April 1941

Today is eighth day since we had the last air-raid alert, but the state of air defence alert is still in force. Since that time the progress of the Hungarian Army towards the Délvidék [Vojvodina] has continued, and it has almost been completed.

As we read it, it is now only a question of overcoming the minor activities of irregular Serbian troops. The interesting fact remains that the diplomatic relations with Yugoslavia have not been broken to this day. Even more remarkable is that the British, who have reasons only due to their friendship with Yugoslavia to do so, have already broken their diplomatic relations with us. It appears that the Yugoslavs, or rather the Serbs, because Croatia announced their "independence" (under German mentorship), have either given up the idea of fighting against us seriously or we have already occupied a large portion of the territory they had seized after Trianon, thus they have difficulty approaching us and hence no more air raids.

The air raid preparations however are still in force, as I mentioned, and I am rostered to sound any alerts. I took over my shift at 5 am. I failed to get the equipment, the armband, and the alarm bell, because my predecessor failed to get it too, also because the person before him forgot to report on duty. So, we do not know who has it. I am not sure if there is another building in Budapest where things are so disorganized.

22 April 1941

Yesterday the streets were lit up, today even the flats were bright. It looks as though—for a short time —we shall have peace and quiet. On the other hand, the call up of the labor servicemen continues, albeit at a slow pace. My brother József was called up last week. Conversely, we also hear of labor servicemen who are discharged. At any event, I am prepared to be called up any minute. Today I entertained the thought that if I am there, we shall amuse ourselves with cultural evenings as happened last year. I wondered what sort of performance I would create. One idea I had was to talk of mathematical curiosities as a philosophical subject. In particular, humanity developing from generation to generation, a continuous existence of humanity, the justifiable selfishness of an individual, and the dilemma between minor or trivial ambitions in life. This is the core of the problem, which we can illustrate only as a problem, without finding a solution.

I once read a philosophical work, which perceived the essence of philosophy precisely in its eternally problematic character. This is perhaps a position leading to disillusionment, but not without some justification.

4 May 1941

I visited Hédi Victor and her family at Pestújhely. This is the first time I called at her flat. The warm family gathering was very agreeable, it is what I had always imagined about their home. As a change compared to my rather arid days, it was truly very refreshing to spend an afternoon there. It was nice to participate again amongst my regular group of friends. My soul, disenchanted with ideals, or at least rather uncertain (I would say torn of ideals), enjoyed this well-grounded family, even looking at it with nostalgia. I feel myself somewhat unworthy of them in my present state. I tried not to think of this. I tried to immerse myself in this fine atmosphere and enjoy Hédi's refinement and kindness, which will serve as an oasis to which I shall return. Naturally, of the whole family Hédi is closest to me, but the family as a whole exudes an immensely charming picture. I managed to create magically a little holiday among my grey, ugly weekdays.

M kir monori 2. honvéd bevonulási központ
Hadigondozó tiszt

100/175. szám.
sgt.hg.- 1943.

       Mult hó 27-én kelt megkérdezésére értesítem, hogy WALDAPFEL LÁSZLÓ /1914.Budapest,anyja:Weisz Anna/ 1942. évi december hó 11-én hadműveleti területen elhunyt. Haláláról közelebbi értesülés híján egyéb közlést nem adhatok.-

Monor, 1943.IV.1.

Pk. mb.

Responding to your inquiry from 27 of the last month I am informing you that LÁSZLÓ WALDAPFEL /1914*, Budapest, mother's name: Anna Weisz/ died on 11 December 1942 in an area of military activity. Lacking further knowledge about the circumstances of his death, I cannot give further information.

Monor, 01.04. 1943.

Military Care Office

The notice by the Army: László Waldapfel died on 11 December 1942, in an area of military activity…

* The correct year of his birth is 1911.

Material Traces

There are no entries dated from August 1940 until April 1941, although the adventure at Badacsony is attested by a post card sent from Révfülöp on the second day. The picture postcards sent from Subcarpathia account for the infomation concerning the months which are missing. During the first period of labor service László was together with his brother Imre. This is the reason the two brothers' names appear numerous times on the postcards sent to the five-year-old son of Imre. After 4 May 1941 the thread is finally lost. From this period only a single greeting, dated Recsk, 29 June 1941 is extant. This informs us that László is spending time with the family of his brother, Gábor. We do not know how long this holiday would last, because soon after the younger brother was called up and dragged off to the area of military activity, from where he did not return.

Gábor also met a tragic end, which he probably did not even anticipate, when, during the first days of his captivity, he was permitted to write to his boss and through him to his own family. As the fate of the brothers has been tied together at many levels, we attach this document to the story of László as well.

Finally, we include another letter, in which the "staggering condemned man," Miklós Radnóti,[37] the greatest Hungarian Jewish poet of the Shoah expresses his condolences to the mourning family, on the passing of László Waldapfel.

"Adolescence is over, and manhood is to begin…"

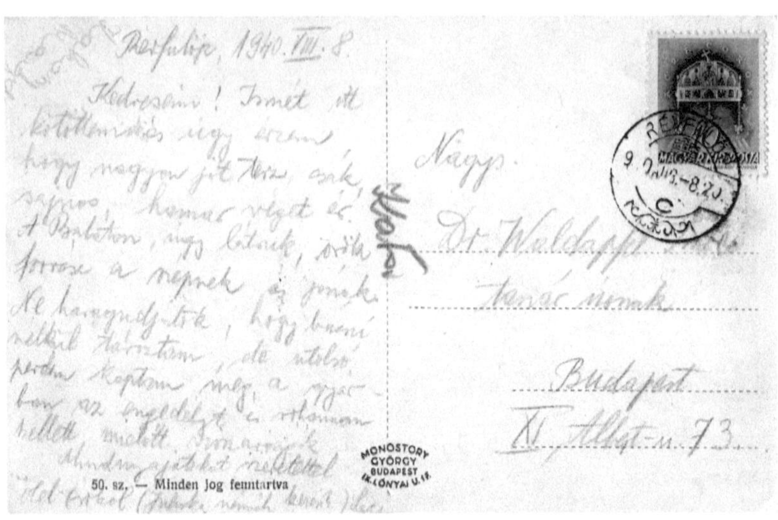

Révfülöp, 08.08. 1940

My Dears! I again ended up here and I feel that it is very good, but unfortunately will end soon. Balaton, it seems, is an eternal source of beauty and goodness. I apologize for having left without saying goodbye, but I got the permission in the factory in the last minute and I had to rush before they withdraw it.

I hug and kiss all of you with love (and I kiss Auntie Juliska's* hands),

Laci.

In the upper left corner of the postcard, the signature of Magda Kakassy (who appears in the entry of 3 October 1935) can be found; we can also deduce that Kata, whose signature runs from top down, must have also belonged among the colleagues from the factory.

* Auntie Juliska is the mother-in-law of Imre Waldapfel.

Weekend at Lake Balaton—most probably with colleagues from
the Weiss Manfréd company.

Comrades from the labor service. Third from right is László,
fourth is his brother, Imre.

The postcard features Hungarian military units entering
Subcarpathia in 1940.

> 8 October 1940.
>
> FROM THE LIBERATED MÁRAMAROSSZIGET
>
> SENDING OUR KISSES
>
> FATHER
>
> and uncle Laci

**To the memory of the liberation of Transylvania. Our army enters Máramarossziget.
5 September 1940
Joint postcard by László and Imre from the labor service, addressed to Imre's five-year old son.**

Work in the Labor Service

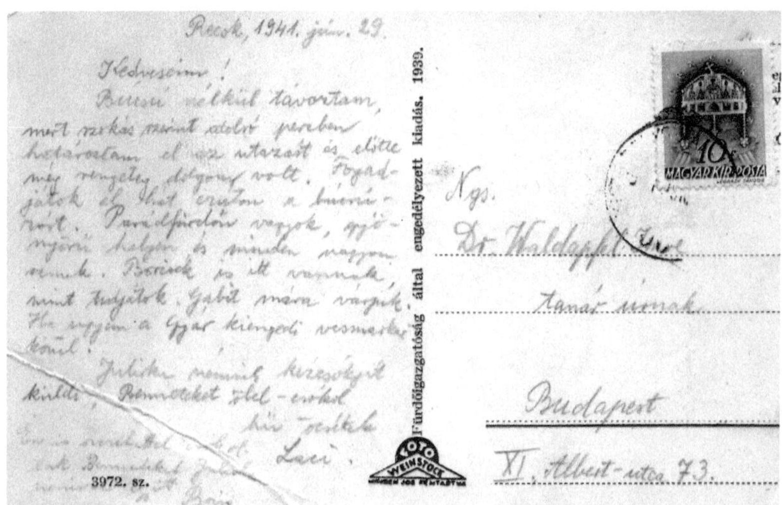

Recsk, 29 June 1941

Dears!

I left without saying goodbye, because, as usual, I decided to leave at the very last moment and I had many things to arrange before the travel. Accept my farewell in this way. I am at Parádfürdő, it is a beautiful place, and everything is excellent. Boris* and her kids are also here, as you know, we expect Gabi to arrive today. If the iron hand of the Factory lets him go.

Kissing the hand of Auntie Juliska and hugging you,

Your true brother,

Laci

The last lifesign from László. Hungary is already at war with the Soviet Union for a week. The mobilization of the labor service was a matter of days...

* Boris is the wife of Gábor.

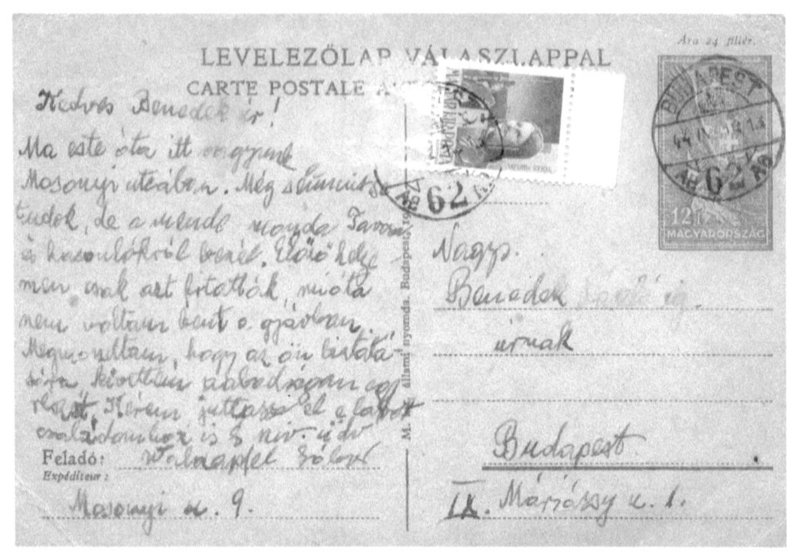

Dear Mr. Benedek!

We have been here since this evening in Mosonyi street.* I know nothing, but the gossip is about Tarcsa and other similar things. In the previous place I was only asked since when I had left the factory. I told them that upon your encouragement I took part of my holidays. Please send this postcard to my family as well, with best regards,

Gábor Waldapfel

Mosonyi street 9.

The last lifesign from Gábor. Open postcard to the director of the company and to his family three weeks after he was arrested. It is not clear who detained him

* Police barracks and prison. Tarcsa (or Kistarcsa) was an infamous internment camp which was also used by Adolf Eichmann and his SS unit in 1944 to prepare the deportation of the Jews from Hungary.

and where was he taken after the Germans occupied
Hungary on 19 March.

My Sweetheart!

I am very worried that I have no news about you. Try to send me a
message at the next visiting day, ask someone to find out when it is.
I have dire need of a cover and some necessary objects, maybe you
can send them with someone. I am finishing and I hope to see you
soon, sending my kisses,

Gabi

11. 04.

The other side of the postcard

> My Dear Imre,
>
> I hope you know that I am with you. What else could I write? Tell this to Eszter and József too. As I was told by Fif,* I will see you on Saturday or Sunday. Until then, I greet you with true love and sympathies, kissing Margit's hands, and a friendly handshake to Imre András,
>
> Miklós
>
> 8 March 1943

Message expressing sympathies to the brothers of László sent by Miklós Radnóti

* Fanni Gyarmati (1912–2014), the wife of Miklós Radnóti.

Küldi: Radnóti Miklós, B. Pozsonyi út 1.II.3.
1943
Nagyságos
Waldapfel Imre dr. tanár, író úrnak,
Budapest, XI.
Albert u 73.

The First Attempt

In the introduction to this volume mention is made of earlier beginnings. The Diary is a continuation of these beginnings, so to speak. Notes from the days of high school are extant—from 1928 August till July 1931, and they illustrate some of the events and László's reflections. The observations of the boy undertaking matriculation and choosing a profession are characteristic of the era of their creation, but a publication of their content in full would "dilute" the essence of the content of the principal text. Therefore, we include only some of the more significant and characteristic portions of the preliminaries.

The Editors

I have been watching the St. Stephen's week festivities at Gellért Hill, just like yesterday and the day before. Today I watched the election of "The Beauty of the Village" and the artistic Olympic Games. The participants in the beauty contest were of diverse quality. There were ugly girls, of whom—if I see them on the street—I would call out "Oh no!" There were some attractive, and a few really pretty ones. People shouted 5's and 8's with great acclaim. Liked number 8 best, if I got that right, a young girl of 13 or 15, with two long black locks of hair, beautiful white teeth, which she showed off with a pleasant smile. I do not know the result.—At the Art Lovers' Olympics, the Society of Artists (quite young children aged 5–12) recited poetry, told jokes and did so happily, enthusiastically, putting their heart and soul into the performance. The leader of the group (I did not note her name), showed especial talent and maturity. She could have been about 7 years old. Little Zsuzsika Baneth, all of 5 years of age, was a great success, reciting poems entiled "A little girl coming from a village to Budapest" and another one of similar genre. I could not stay until the end.

Slightly improved and copied, I sent the letter I wrote a week or two ago to the editor of Néptanítók Lapja [The Village Teachers' Journal]. It is about the reunions to be held after graduation for those who had to repeat a school year. I wonder if the editor will publish my initiative; and if he does, I wonder what effect it will have among the appropriate circles: the village teachers?

25 December 1928

Today I became 17 years old. I have been thinking about this once earlier, at the time of the counting of Omer.[38] 17 years is somehow an age, that is not often referred to, it symbolizes nothing. When I realized that I shall be 17 years old, I was almost astonished. This figure was so unfamiliar. It is not discussed like e.g., 18 or 20, or any of the preceding ones (from 13). I understand that, at least in my case. This is the age when we are not noisy, only preparing silently for our life. Adolescence is over, and manhood is to begin. We become serious, no longer demanding, and we do not repeat loudly our aims and ideas, as in adolescence. We immerse ourselves in thinking about what we can do after matriculation. The last minute!

We must delve heavily into the problems of choosing a path to a profession, and the ethical problems related to this must be taken into account. I am agonizing about this most of the time, and hope I shall succeed in finding a profession which is most suitable to serve both my happiness and links it to the public interest.

In order to assure the accuracy of my Diary, I recount the "harvest" arising from my birthday. Gabi gave me a book even before the day, by Gábor Oláh: *Petőfi's Imagination*. On the birthday, my father[39] presented me with Mousson's *Physics* in three volumes, two Christmas supplements of *Pesti Hírlap*, and a novel by Max Brand: *The Trail of the Panther*. Eszti gave me a necktie, Imre[40] promised me a radio, Jóska[41] and family visited me in the evening and gave me a volume of Dickens, containing *A Christmas Carol* and *Hard Times*.

---

3 February 1929

How remarkably a person's perception can change about certain things! Their understanding develops slowly. During the turmoils and stirring an appropriate view of world is formed, as well as an appropriate view of humanity, and I hope that an understanding of ethics and morals is formed as well. Because a permanent anxiety must be destructive. First, I thought that by becoming a teacher, I shall earn a good income, and I will found a school.

I continue to think of a good income, but from a different viewpoint. This time the reason is that I could support those who are poor as a result of natural causes or the injustice imposed by society. Today I even considered that I must not aim for a teaching position with a low income because that would not enable me to exercise charity to a reasonable degree. On the other hand, it would be a great sacrifice, to give up a profession, which attracts me. In the final analysis, the results of my deliberations lead to the conclusion that a person is selfish to a certain degree, he has the right to be selfish, and therefore he is not obliged to give up a material well-being purely because there exist others who cannot aspire to such well-being. This is where I stand tonight, but with an anxious soul. The turmoil has not abated and may not cease for long time yet.

---

20 February 1929

Yesterday Dr Pruzsinszky,[42] the director, brought along a book for my father, to read and discuss afterwards. The author is Olivér Hazay, and the title of the book is A book for teachers, parents, and pupils. (NB it was published in 1910). It awakened my interest (in spite of everything I am some sort of pedagogue—or I will be...) and I started to read the book. I read the introduction which is largely an allegorical tale about the soul of the child. Then I read the next chapter, which discusses the relationship between teacher and pupil. Or it does not. The grandiose word "discuss" does not fit in here. Olivér Hazay does not "discuss," he merely thinks about, feels, and expresses his thoughts and feelings. We cannot even call different parts of the book by the name of chapters, they are separate musings over the souls of children. These few pages truly awaken a warm sympathy, and are soul-lifting, educational as well as serving to educate the teachers. I cannot be certain whether I shall finish reading the book, but I would like to do so, and it would be desirable.

17 March 1929

Sunday. A Sunday in March. It is true that March so far did not mean what it usually means. But today, when I looked out of the window, I saw springtime weather. But only looking out of the window. Although it was Sunday, a Sunday in March. A Sunday in Spring. And I so much desired to enjoy it. I can so much enjoy a nice Sunday afternoon. I feel joy as well as pain at this time on the street. The streets are full of life and excitement. And I live the life of other people. It is a joy that I am alive, but a pain that I live the lives of others... Today I had so fervently wished to be in the blessed sunshine, to live the life of the springtime Sunday, to smell thousands of aromas, to observe and to enjoy the thousand colours of nature... But I am coughing and thus I cannot leave my home... Oh this terrible body which hinders the happiness of the soul!... This is how the pessimists used to speak in such cases... But I do not say this. Silly talk! When the body permits one to enjoy life, does it not convey this joy? It partly transmits the enjoyment and does it not increase it by bodily beauty, does it not accompany and frame it exquisitely? One may despair, one may be sad about the lost Sunday in March, but one cannot complain because of it.

Today I took part in a mathematics quest at the school, which was designed to decide who should be chosen to go to the national mathematics competition from our institution. We had to solve three problems. I solved the first two but could not complete the third one because I ran out of time. Two competitors, Görgey from our class and Bartók from Class B finished a lot earlier than I did. I spoke to Bartók.

I do not think he solved the first problem properly (he certainly did it differently to me), I think I did well and feel almost certain that my solution is correct. We shall see when the results come out.

I found out that I failed the mathematics quest, there will be another contest between the two students, Bartók and Görgey. It seems that I solved the first problem wrongly after all, and this decided my results. Although I do not regard these problems suitable that, on the basis of these results, they could decide who should or should not go to the national mathematics competition. Namely one can understand the question in a certain way, the way I solved it, but finally I have to admit that the other solution is correct.

I have been alone almost the whole summer, so I had time to do some thinking. I have thought about things related to the choice of a career. I got bored with all the thinking, my soul got tired of being tossed about, I would like to enjoy some peace.

I do not know when the final tranquillity will set in, but for the moment I am determined to put my worries to sleep; perhaps this will allow me to have a better perspective. However, in order that this lulling should not mean that my conscience has gone totally to sleep, and in order to rethink it all, today I felt that there are still some problems to be solved. That is why I wrote these lines. This means that the problem has not been dealt with and it becomes more pressing. For the time being I shall enroll at the Faculty of Arts for the third semester, as a maths/physics student, a member of the Teachers Training Institute.

19 July 1931

Does classical literature have any impact at all, beyond an aesthetic effect? Does it have some moral effects, a quietening effect on the soul, a guideline to the conduct of life? Will I find a settling of my soul in the midst of frequent turmoils I keep experiencing? Even if not a totally calming effect, at least an idea which could start off a correct way to conduct my life in a moral manner, which has already been jeopardized? I read currently the following passage in the novel entitled Black Bridegrooms by Irén P. Gulácsy: "he allowed himself to be embraced by a warmth which overwhelmed him in its surging, triumphant thrill, so that it could be described as a pure joy.—'Well, this is the life for others!'. He heard his voice cry out, from somewhere very far away." These lines refer to Imre Czibak, whose life was a great disappointment, and who lost all hope. I have read these lines in such a way that I had a feeeling as though a sudden spark had struck me.

This is the end of the first diary. We found a further two drafts for newspaper articles amongst the archives of László. These highlight further the richness of thought and emotions experienced by this young intellectual born in an evil era.

Poor People

I am sitting on a bench in the beautiful sunshine, in the vicinity of a convent. When I walk around here at midday, I often observe men, women, and children of various ages, carrying pots and spoons, waiting in front of the convent. At other times I see them waiting in the courtyard of the convent, scooping the food prepared by the nuns for the poor people.

As I said, I am sitting near the convent when suddenly I see a group of small boys running towards the building. There would have been about six of them, holding hands in pairs: an older boy and a toddler. They all try to run quickly, their little legs can barely keep up, but they persist. The small boys, aged 4–5, all know they must keep up. Their faces have a serious expression. These boys do not play now, they are struggling already, partaking in the pressing battle of life, and they look ahead with all seriousness: they are men already. Poor little men! They take things seriously, they run with determination because they feel that they must run. Yes, they must! One of them shouts: Ili, let us hurry! It is half past twelve already!

The smaller boys try even harder. The older ones assist the smaller ones, but the latter do not complain. One of them approaches the pavement and already he can see the gate of the convent. (It is closed.) He tells this to the others in a horrified voice.

This seriousness touches my heart. The struggle of a small boy for his existence. They know that perhaps they will miss out on their lunch and may remain hungry until midday tomorrow…

Are there such beginnings to life?! Very well, let them suffer, everybody suffers to receive the joys life has to offer, and for these joys it is worth undergoing suffering. But will these children be rewarded for putting up their serious fight, and for their mother's suffering, with a better life?

Because everyone who was born to this earth, and for whom a mother has suffered, has the right to a happy life!

László Waldapfel

Text written with a typewriter, on the reverse side a complex mathematical problem.

Technocracy in Art

The journal Pester Lloyd reported a strange news item from Paris. They put the Venus de Milo, the world-renowned treasure of the Louvre—the reason for the pilgrimage of people worshipping art, and the admirers of the beauty of human body—on a turntable made of marble. They did so in order that the public could admire the statue from all sides comfortably, without having to walk around it. The reader who is in touch with art spiritually, winces at reading this news. He finds the idea at first interesting, but immediately notes that it is grotesque, and suddenly it dawns on him that what happened is a murder. They killed a great artistic creation and they have mutilated a great artistic experience. Has the person, in whose brain this idea arose, got any clue about the essence of sculpture, has he heard of the essence of the Greek gods, and has he any idea of the methods of appreciation of fine art? Is it not one of the essential features of sculptures that they are rigid and yet in their rigidity they are still able to express life? And the Greek Goddess, does she not represent one of the eternal forces, way above us, with her permanence, great calm, and yet resembling a being, similar to humans? From now on the Venus de Milo will be comparable to the tailor's dummies, which revolve around at fashion parades, offering their figures—or rather the clothes they are dressed in and whose promotion is their reason for existing. Is it possible to enjoy the beauty of a statue as it revolves in front of me like someone in delirium? It revolves—lit up theatrically, and I must keep to its tempo in order to view it, dictated by an overly clever, yet stupid mechanism. Do the directors of the Louvre appreciate that that all sensitive artistic experience has been lost which had been associated with viewing the statue of Venus de Milo? Another technical trick, which as technical step provides nothing new—after all steadily revolving movements are classed amongst the simplest of technical tasks. They killed an artistic experience, which is part of the common treasure of humanity, an artistic creation from a great epoch. It could have fulfiled its most excellent calling, and now it misses the point, and gets enrolled in the service of infernal destruction. The frequently and often unjustly criticized technology has in this instance truly disgraced itself.

László Waldapfel

Handwritten, carefully proofed text. The date is clear from the letter from the journal editors, see the picture.

Szám 5015.   Budapest, 193 6 május 25.

Reklamáció esetén szí-
veskedjék a fenti számra
hívatkozni.

                    Igen tisztelt tanár ur.

        vis cikkében nagyon helyes érveket sorakoztatott fe
fel, de - ugy hisszük - a francia müvészek is alapo-
san megvitatták ezt a kérdést. cikkét nem közöljük,
mert feltétlenül pro és contra hozzászókások egész se-
regével keresnének fel, már pedig a különböző véle-
nyek közlésére, a vita kimélyitésére nincs helyünk.
Kivánságát igy - sajnálatunkra - nem teljesithetjük.

                                      Tisztelettel

                        A PESTI HIRLAP szerkesztősége.

Number 5015.

Budapest 25 May 1936

Honoured Professor,

You have marshalled some very appropriate reasons, however, we believe that the French artists have also discussed this question in depth. We shall not publish your article, because we would be inundated with a host of comments both for and against, and we lack the space to publish all the varied opinions and to drag this debate any further. Thus, with regret, we are unable to fulfil your wishes.

Faithfully,

The editorial team of Pesti Hírlap

(signature)

Notes

...what is not clarified by the
text of the original source

In the following, we make an attempt to uncover as far as possible the network around László Waldapfel. The generally well-known historical figures (statesmen, leaders, politicians) do not require elaboration, but we provide some form of guidelines to the relative positions of the lesser-known persons in this life-story.

We had the greatest difficulties identifying persons in his private life and in close contacts, although their recollection seems to be most vital for understanding the references in the Diary. Our presentation follows the order of their appearance in the text.

1   **István Benkő jr.** (1889–1959): Benkő's career commenced during a special period of the Reformed Church. During this period there developed within the Church a reform movement which was aimed at a generational change in the composition of the higher-level priesthood, and a reduction or removal of social injustices. Benkő himself belonged among those priests who worked hard to achieve a change in the generational struc-

ture, a wider inclusion of youth, and evangelization of the student bodies. He enrolled in the students' movement in 1912, and he edited the paper known as the "Students' World." The First World War however broke up the ranks of the movement, because many were called up to military service.

Benkő's sensitivity towards the poor and his desire to become active after the catastrophic war brought him in contact with the communist government in 1919. After the suspension of the Reformed Presbyterium, on 30 March 1919, he announced that the proletarian members of the congregation at Újfalu formed a church directorium. At the beginning of April, he made a speech at the church in Ráday Street, which was later labelled to be of "communist flavor." Benkő drew a parallel between Christian brotherhood and the concept of brotherhood in socialism. He warned, however, that whilst the new order looks at this concept as an institution, the Bible treats humans as soul-mates. After the Soviet Republic failed, he was arraigned before the Church court. Finally, they condemned him to some "disapproval," the mildest disciplinary punishment, which had not influenced his future path negatively. He continued to work as the head of the congregation in Rákospalota. He became a prelate in 1938, published numerous articles and participated in the activities of various societies and editorial groups.

Sources: Budapest blog, XV. district, Rákospalota, Pestújhely, Újpalota blogs of local history

2 **Pro Christo Student Association**: this was a significant local branch of the so called "Awakening Movements," which originated in the nineteenth century; a pietist stream seeking to counter the process of secularization and wishing to confront the social and spiritual distortions in society with the Gospels, i.e., the spirit of Christs's teachings. Focusing on the youth, it attempted to return the evangelist civil movements to

the (in its mainstream socially and politically conservative) official Church structures. This "reintegration" was semi-successful, thanks to a number of "apostolic" personalities, such as, amongst others, István Benkő, János Victor jr. and, last but not least, Sándor Karácsony, who all challenged this conservative mainstream in different ways.

3 **Pál Selényi** (born Pál Schlesinger, 1884–1954): one of the greatest and most versatile researchers of Hungarian experimental physics. His inventions and patents are of international significance. During the 1919 Soviet Republic, he was appointed professor in experimental physics. He had to pay a high price for this as after the fall of the communist regime he was forbidden to hold any state employment and could only find employment with a private firm. From 1921 he worked in the research laboratories of Egyesült Izzó (United Electrics), inventing many new technologies.

4 **Hédi Victor** (1910–2005): her name appears for the first, but not the last time in the diary, on New Year's Eve, 1933. Her identification caused the greatest concern for the editors. It is clear that her figure appeared significant in the spiritual and physical eyes of this young man who was looking for his place in society. Clearly, he would have liked to have been able to rise to her status. We know that a girl bearing that name was born in 1910, according to the archives of the Veress Pálné High School. She lived until 2005. She was most probably attending university classes together with László, born in 1911. Her name appears in the 1950 edition of the telephone directory of Budapest, with the address given as XIVth district, 4. Erzsébet Királyné Road, and designated as a chemist/physicist. In an interview with János Victor, Jr., a minister of the Reformed Church, the name of Aunt Hédi is mentioned en passant, who had worked in the Egyesült Izzó company as a physicist. In the genealogy of this

notable family, of numerous generations of clergymen, amongst the numerous children of Ágoston Victor there appears a girl called Hédi, without dates of birth (geni.com). Ágoston himself was not an insignificant personality, but his brother János (1860–1956) played an even more important role in the history of the Victor family and in Hungarian public life. He was a leader of the Deaconess Institute, secretary of the Society of Sunday Schools, later its President, and editor of its journal. His son was János Victor jr. (1888–1954), clergyman, teacher of theology, editor of newspapers, secretary of the Hungarian Evangelical Christian Students Society. In 1944 he was saving the lives of Jewish friends and members of his congregation of Jewish ethnic origin. He and his wife received the title of Righteous Among the Nations for their rescuing efforts. It is clear that the intellectual and moral commitments of the Victor family played an important role for the milieu of our diary-writer. Through an excerpt one can get a glimpse of the progressive protestant spirituality, combining social commitment and ecumenism with eschatological overtones, linked to the Scandinavian Awakening movement, which affected the circle László belonged to:

[...] The Finnish man Pål Routsalainen lived a hundred years ago. He was a farmer. He was the Finnish "Peasant prophet"... He was placed by God at the head of that great religious movement, which renewed the life of the Finnish people, like the Reformation for us.

The title speaks of a Hungarian Routsalainen. We do not wish to simply copy the Finnish Peasant Prophet for our use. Perhaps whomever God may send to us with a mission similar to Pål's will not be a peasant, but a person from the middle class, and his tasks may not be identical. He may be a single person or a group of people. All we mean by this comment that we wish fervently that God delivers to us Hungarians somebody or more than one person who would possess heavenly powers, so that as a result of his visible activities and the re-birth of certain people and small communities there could be a renewal mobilizing the whole Hungarian nation. [...]

Perhaps God does not grant us this awakening, which so many of us desire and expect, because we only ask for an awakening and no more. Not only the awakening of many, many individuals, but that of the whole people, the renewal of his Church, Reformation. [...] Churches, groups of people, societies, movements, Bible circles co-exist side by side in profusion, and they regard, separately, their service to be the only true instrument of awakening. The numerous individual, separate circles is the punishment meted out for our errors. It cannot be relieved by some over-reaching great organization. Only if we repent, may God help us that there be unity in all separation: a community which can carry the Sacred Soul of God.

Source: *János Victor, jr:* A magyar Routsalainen Pál előszobájában. *[In the anteroom of the Hungarian Pål Routsalainen]. In:* A másik ember. Az Exodus almanachja *[The other man. The Almanach of the Exodus], 1940.*

5 **Pál Vidor** (1908?–1945?): somewhat differing accounts indicate that he was born in 1908 or 1909, and died in 1945 in the concentration camp of Buchenwald. According to some recollections, he could have escaped the deportation but refused to leave his community alone. He completed his university studies in the Rabbinical Seminary and in the Péter Pázmány University, Budapest. He was ordained a Rabbi on 22 March 1932. Closer to our theme we observe his activities as a leader of boy scouts.

The spiritual attitude of Jewish boy scouts is perhaps best illustrated by the following recollection:

An Opening Speech written for the Memorial Ceremony of the 311 Vörösmarty Boy Scout Group

We of the Vörösmarty Group had four identities. We are Hungarians, Jews, Scouts, and finally from the Vörösmarty group. Depending on how many members there have been, they have all been dominated in their soul by the many different identities. The most important, and most all-embracing identity has been the Vörösmarty identity. We have been Hungarians, since we were born here, have lived here,—as long as they let us—we walked along its land, we collected the songs of the Hungarian nation and we have sung them. This has been our homeland and for many it remains that today. There have been those who were more attached or less attached to all this. We were Jews, because we were born Jewish, we shared all its joyful aspects and its sorrows, we listened to the teachings of our fathers or rather of our grandfathers and we had participated in the high holiday ceremonies with reverence or skepticism. When fate dictated, we bore our suffering with fortitude. We had amongst us Godfearing people and atheists, but we respected each others' beliefs and ways of life. We have been scouts, after all we knew and respected the ten laws of the scouts. We have learnt, taught, and enjoyed all the intellectual and physical knowledge that was represented by being a boy scout. We adhered firmly to the rules of our games, and we strove to win. It caused a great happiness for us to have a shared tradition and conventions, a discipline accepted willingly. Some liked it more, some less. People liked scouting for various reasons. There was however an identity, which differed from all others: to be from the Vörösmarty group. The other major component of this identity has been a sense of humor, the irony and self-irony. We said that whoever cannot laugh at himself has no right to laugh at anyone else. This humor could become cruel at times, as the young are cruel, but those who accepted it and returned it in kind, never abandoned the other. Finally, undeniably, this identity was deeply based on human culture and human learning. We entertained, not only ourselves with the yearly performances and lectures, but acquired the finest gems of poetry and literature, which we then passed on to others.

Source: zsidoiskolasok.tk.mta.hu – *the meeting was held on 20 October 2000*

6   **Pejsli**: Lung stew, from German/Yiddish *Beuschel*.

7   **Gyula Kornis** (1885–1958): piarist priest, philosopher, educational and cultural politician, university professor. His writings in the 1910s attested to his psychological sensitivity and broad horizons of knowledge. As President of the Hungarian Pedagogical Society as well as the High School Teachers' Training Committee, he was in direct personal contact with László Waldapfel's father. As a result of the traumatic political events in 1918–19, he became a staunch supporter of the ruling conservative ("Christian-national") ideology. He continued to participate extensively in the cultural institutions of the country, serving also as President of the Academy of Sciences.

As historian of psychology György Hunyady put it:

He was conservative, defending the cultural traditions of his class and the hierarchic structure of society against all varieties of radicalism and even against the democratic mobilization of society. His instruments were knowledge and reason and, using these means, he extolled the glory of sentiment and values ... On the basis of his idealism and conservatism he consistently denied racial theories and, believing in the rule of law, he confronted dictatorship and its local epigons.

Source: *György Hunyady:* Kornis Gyula szellemi és közéleti pályafutása *[The intellectual and public career of Gyula Kornis], in* Tanulmányok a Magyar Pedagógiai Társaság történetéből *[Studies from the history of the Hungarian Pedagogic Society], ed. by László Trencsényi, Budapest, Hungarian Pedagogic Society, 2016.*

8   **Ágnes Zombory** (1910–2001): she came from an Eastern Hungarian intellectual family of Protestant clergymen, and was active in the Hungarian Evangelic Christian Student Association. In 1932 she married Richárd Bodoky (1908–1996) pastor of the Diaconess Institute, and became his committed companion in organizing the training of Protestant women for social service, especially in hospitals and orphanages. Her husband came from a Hungarianized Swiss-Austrian family of pastors (Biberauer), who took the Hungarian family name in the 1940s. He studied both in Lutheran and Calvinist secondary schools and then started the theological studies in the moment when the conflict of "historical Calvinism" and ecumenic Christian trends escalated. He opted for the position of János Victor, a key figure of the latter stream. The Bodoky family, together with the Diaconesses, were also involved in saving Jews during the Holocaust, fabricating false papers, and hiding orphaned children. Beyond these biographical facts we can also add more colorful details as during our search for information we luckily met their daughter, Ágnes Bodoky, who kindly provided us with the memoirs of her father, which gives an excellent picture not only of the personalities of her parents but also the cultural and

political atmosphere of the 1930s. We quote here from the following scene:

> *(...) It happened that the girls form the Student Association were quite numerous in this mathematical seminar (...) and naturally Ágnes was there as well. If something needed to be organized and there was a need to act, she was always quickly finding the way. So, she was widely popular in this interesting group not only because of her external beauty but also for this organizing capacity. (...)*
>
> *And there was a need to act not only once. Usually, the events started around the grape harvest season (...) which were described in the press, if they happened to write about them at all, in terms of "disturbances at the university." (...) Members of the Association of Awakening Hungarians and other anti-Semitic groupings chanted anti-Jewish rallying cries and beat up some Jewish students. Naturally only boys, as during the conservative Christian Course the self-praise of "cultural superiority" was pleasing itself with re-iterating the "chivalric character" of Hungarians. (...)*
>
> *Maybe it was exactly the girls from the Christian Student Association who organized a counteraction. And then they were joined by other female students. They quickly herded their Jewish colleagues into the corner of a classroom and by standing closely next to each other formed a wall around them which could not be broken up by the "chivalric" Kémeri [Imre Kémeri Nagy, 1903–1942, an extremist student leader] and his followers. They were furious. They were cursing not only the Jews but also castigated the unpatriotic behavior of the girls protecting them.*

Source: Richárd Bodoky: Szent Mihály napja – Családtörténeti töredékek (1928–1932) *[Day of Saint Michael – Fragments of family history, 1928–1932]. Edited by Ágnes Bodoki, published by Bodoky Richárd's Heirs, Budapest, 2007.*

We would like to thank Ms. Csanády Andrásné Ágnes Bodoky for the valuable information.

9 **Sándor Karácsony** (1891–1952): born into a family of Calvinist farmers and pastors, he was a multifarious intellectual and organizer. Due to an injury during WWI, his physical movement was limited, which he compensated for with remarkable intellectual mobility. He worked in many different disciplinary fields, such as psychology, linguistics, ethnography, theology, and anthropology. He was also involved in practical pedagogy as a literature teacher and a boy scout leader, and also acted as a journal editor. Not even touching on his philosophical, linguistic, and socio-political achievements, we only highlight one aspect of his sparkling personality, which created a common wavelength between the master and his pupils. We quote the pedagogue, using his own words from the period László interacted with him:

When an individual matures from a child to an adult, the maturation process can be measured accurately from time to time, using another person. Infant, growing child, adolescent, and youth discover and accept another person from an eccentric point of view. The other person is either a hindrance or an instrument for the Ego to succeed. The relationship of the developing person to the other person is simple and almost unmistakable: he overcomes, as far as he can, the hindrance, and makes use of the assistance. The individual may be regarded as an adult when he first becomes aware of the truth that the other person is an au-

tonomous being and he then adjusts himself to this fact. It is not the 24 years of existence which indicates whether somebody is mature or not, but it is those gestures, which due to their character betray whether the individual respects the autonomy of the other person.

It is no different in the life of the community. A cultural group may initially behave from the point of view of another community as a child. It is like a growing child, later undergoing puberty, then exhibiting adolescent behavior. However, it only reaches the zenith of development, and can only be regarded as a mature community, if within its confines one person, in all aspects of activity, respects the autonomy of the other person. Showing this respect can be demonstrated by several means. I regard every common achievement a fruit of our joint labor.

Source: Magyar nevelés *[Hungarian education] in: Sándor Karácsony, Magyarság és nevelés. Válogatott tanulmányok [Hungarianness and education. Selected studies], Budapest, Áron Kiadó, 2003.*

As for the Bible-circle mentioned in the text, we cannot identify with absolute certainty the group in question. Judging by Miklós Heltai's presence in the Diary, we may deduce that we are speaking of the Exodus editorial working group, which was started initially as a Bible-circle. A question, which needs to be solved, is how a young man of Jewish background, possessing a mathematics-physics teacher's diploma, working as an employee in an office, finds himself in this circle – although he undoubtedly had strong philosophical and social-psychology related and pedagogic interests, which were central to Karácsony's work as well.

10 **Miklós Heltai** (1909 – 1989): he appears as an author, together with Sándor Karácsony and János Victor in the second *Exodus Almanach* (1940), entitled "The other man." Although his writing here is not so much philosophical, but rather of a didactic character, there can be no doubt that he has been the representative of the more liberal train of thought within the Calvinist intelligentsia. We only know, from the scant information provided, that he was a history teacher and local geographer in Gödöllő. (We also have information that as a university student he had been in more or less friendly contact with László's older brother, Imre, and his future wife, Margit Petrolay). His son, Miklós Heltai jr. was baptized by Sándor Karácsony. His valuable contribution is referred to in two citations connected to the Museum at Gödöllő:

> *[...] The City Museum of Gödöllő is situated in the center of the town, in an aristocratic building, built in the 1760s. The collection's basis was provided by the association of local history, founded in 1952 by Miklós Heltai (1909–1989). [...]*

Source: www.artportal.hu/lexikon

> *[...] In the museum operating in one of the oldest buildings in town, a welcoming atmosphere greets the visitor. The exhibitions depict how the original Protestant farmers, the immigrant Catholic artisans, and the Jewish merchants, as well as the intellectuals and the artists enriched and formed the town's scenery. (...) The materials of the museum at the beginning were collected by Miklós Heltai, a teacher of history, with his students.*

Source: www.museumap.com/gvm

11 **Erzsébet Hirschberg** (1911?–?): the mention of an "unpleas-ant conversation" in the diary entry, dated 1 April 1934, suggests that the mutual agreement with Bözsi Hirschberg was generally important for László. This time the issue related to a certain Winkler, about whom Bözsi and László disagreed. We believe that it may refer to an aged professor of chemistry (Lajos Winkler, 1863–1939). Under the name Erzsébet Hirschberg, we found a dance artist. With regard to her, the following lines appear in a study on the history of eurhythmics, quoting her autbiography:

According to my father the future belonged to chemistry and physics. Therefore, I enrolled at the University to the faculty of physics and chemistry. As a student, I became obliged to join in the activities of BEAC (University Athletics Club of Budapest). I took part in the training sessions with great enthusiasm, and I got acquainted at training with Hédi Victor, and later with her whole family. Our friendship has been unbroken to this day. [This interview was made in 1980 – The Editors]. Hédi's physical build was similar to mine. She became my gymnastics partner. Both of us achieved selection for the Olympic squad. We entered many gymnastics competitions. I worked incredibly hard, beyond the compulsory lessons and laboratory exercises. [...]. In the spring of 1934, I met Valéria Dienes. This meeting spurred me on to my further dancing activities. On 29 April as a member of the Olympic squad I participated in the gymnastics exhibition held at the City Theatre with Hédi Victor—performing paired acrobatics and exercises on the bar. In May we performed again in two of Auntie Valéria's performances, entitled Ten Virgins and the Saint of Roses. They were mystery plays. The second one took place at the time of the canonization of St Elizabeth. Meantime I submitted my request

*to the Teachers' Training College to pass the closing exam-
ination in Philosophy and Pedagogy. On 29 September
1939 I took the examinations in philosophy under Ágost
Pauler and Gyula Kornis and the same in pedagogy under
professor Prohászka. Finally, I obtained the diploma to
become a high school teacher. [...]*

Source: *Erzsébet Hirschberg:* A tánc szerepe életemben *[The role
of dancing in my life]. In: Julia Lenkei:* A mozdulatművészet
Magyarországon *[Movement art in Hungary], Veszprém, Pannon
Egyetemi Kiadó, 2004.*

12 **Gábor Waldapfel** (1902–1944?): László's oldest brother. He
belonged to the leadership group of the Globus Canning Factory,
a firm of the Weiss Manfréd industrial complex. He was arrested immediately after the German occupation of Hungary on 19
March 1944, in order to gain important information about the
acquisition of the firm in the context of the competition between the SS and the Hungarian state to capture the assets of
the company, now well-documented from several sources. We
do not know the exact date, location and circumstances of his
death, one reference points to Süttő, a station of the death
march organized by the Arrow Cross government to the
Austrian border.

13 A famous ballad by the Hungarian poet, János Arany, written in 1857, about the self-sacrificial heroism of the **Welsh Bards**,
refusing to praise the conquering English King Edward I.

14 **Béla Brandenstein** (1901 – 1989): philosopher, university
professor. After attending the Budapest Teachers' Training
College, he completed his doctorate in philosophy in 1923, and
became Professor in 1934, and from 1938 to 1944 President of
the Hungarian Philosophical Society. After 1945 he lived first in

Austria and then became professor at the University of Saarbrücken. We learn more about his attitudes from his press statement, also referred to in the Diary:

Béla Brandenstein rejects the baseless attacks against the University Social Research Institute

One of the liberal evening newspapers published an article by Géza Féja, entitled an "Arrow Cross leader lectures at the University." In this article, the paper directs a sharp attack against Baron Béla Brandenstein, a University Professor, for having invited Kálmán Hubay, a member of parliament, to give a lecture to the seminar which is under his leadership at the Social Research Institute. Géza Féja in his article instructs the eminent professor that one must not drag politics into the realm of the University, stating that Kornis "would not have conducted the Social Research Institute in this spirit."

This conspicuous attack which targeted one of the great figures of Hungarian science, created a general uproar, since it has been known that Baron Brandenstein's work is far distant from daily politics and the aim of the Institute and its work to date is independent of all daily politics and serves the higher educational aims of the nation. We therefore asked Professor Baron Brandenstein in connection with the lecture by Hubay about the extent to which the accusations by the left-wing paper correspond to the truth.

– I had an opportunity – said Professor Brandenstein to read the article by Géza Féja, which appeared in Magyarország. With regard to its content, I can state the following. The social research seminar, which has been largely, but not entirely under my leadership is not strictly speaking a university seminar, but a more open scientific organization, which operates under the supervision, be-

sides me, of Antal Schütz and Farkas Heller, but I am responsible for the immediate direction. Precisely this is the reason why the lectures are conducted in the philosophical seminary and I notify the dean of any special circumstances. Géza Féja is correct in pointing out that, as he cites from our conversations at this venue, people of all different world views have spoken. For instance, this year Antal Schütz and Kálmán Csathó held meetings. Regarding the Jewish question, I myself asked László Waldapfel to give a lecture. At another lecture delivered by the German writer Kurt Wohldran, at my request Count György Széchenyi also added his comment.

– At the meeting on 6 May, Kálmán Hubay gave a lecture. At these meetings, in line with the nature of the seminary, not only students but also grown-ups participate. Thus at Hubay's lecture many university teachers and other eminent people have turned up. The procedure at these meetings is that the lecturer expresses his ideas in a strictly objective manner, and all participants are fully free to present their opinion in an objective and courteous manner. This is followed by a reply from the speaker and I speak on the note of closing the meeting. We deal deliberately with contemporary social and cultural matters because I am convinced that in a civilized society individuals of the most contrary views must be able to express their point of view face to face, with measured arguments.

This process, in my view is the only suitable way that, in today's clashes of the most diverse ideological streams, we could avoid the development of physical violence in the conflicts of spiritual ideas, and thus avert the threatening dangers to the national society inherent in a violent confrontation. I espoused this opinion in the leading article which appeared in Új Magyarság last Thursday. I am not betraying a secret when I tell you that my attitude was not formed just yesterday. I wrote it at the beginning of March, before the program of Győr.

The youth do not become influenced in any way by a one-sided political opinion. This is guaranteed by the possibility of free rein given to the most diverse political views. This is what I try to secure in my closing remarks. I need not speak about my views too much as I imagine they are generally well-known from my writings and lectures. This Weltanschauung, which I have presented to the public for the past fourteen years, did not require any adjustment, in spite of the numerous local and world events which had occurred.

Naturally we can always question the veracity of anything said by a person, perhaps they might think different things compared to what has been said. We cannot look into their hearts. I can only say about myself that I live by my convictions that in the final analysis not only our actions but also our words and deeds are known before the Eternal Truth and they will be made known for all of us to see. Thus I strive not only to speak but also to think like this.

– Géza Féja in his article mentions that Kálmán Hubay entered the antechamber, with a slogan "Courage!" [i.e., the greeting of the Arrow Cross movement – The Editors] This implies a simple propagandistic act. What is your opinion about this view?

– I can only comment that Kálmán Hubay did not enter and shout "Courage!", he adhered to the rules of the Social Research Institute and emphasized that he is not involving politics in the context of his speech. Essentially, he spoke about the characterology of the development of the Zeitgeist, not of the spirit of the current age. Everybody who had attended would have noticed, myself included, that his lecture contained neither implicit nor virulent propaganda. One cannot raise any scientific objections against his

sketch of social characterology. I must emphasize that I communicated this to Géza Féja personally.

– I think, – concluded Professor Brandenstein – that in today's schism of world views it would be desirable that our Hungarian society embraced the idea that we need not be afraid of seriously debating completely opposing views, but such a debate must be conducted in the spirit of mutual respect towards our opponents and in a true Christian spirit. Only such a deeply ingrained Christian spirit can assure the survival of the Hungarian nation in the period of deep turmoil, and the achievement of its well-deserved spiritual greatness.

The above statement by the professor, responding to the left-wing agrarian writer's article published in the journal *Magyarország*, came to light in special circumstances. It forms part of a more extensive, edited piece, which appeared in a virulently right-wing paper, immediately after the voting on the "first anti-Jewish Law" in the Upper House, evidently meant to justify these laws. Already the title reflected the spirit of the piece: *"Béla Imrédy: In the case of Jews the racial element shows itself sharply; assimilation is difficult to achieve."* After the interview with Brandenstein the journal added an interview with László Endre, an infamous anti-Semite, who in 1944 was to play a key role in the deportation of Jews from Hungary. Here he is talking about *"left-wing press terror and false news."* In this textual and political environment one can see better the ambiguity of Baron Brandenstein's words... It needs to be added that László continued to participate in the circle of Brandenstein, as attested by the 1942 publication of the journal *Athenaeum*, reporting the debate organized by the Hungarian Philosophical Association around a lecture by György Zemplén on *"Metaphysics*

and the theory of values," where among the printed comments
we see both his name and Brandenstein's.

15 The brother of Kálmán Hubay (Kálmán Hubay was a noto-
rious extreme right-wing member of Parliament, executed after
the war): the person under consideration was most probably
Sándor Hubay. Several threads of information are attached to
this name, but closest to the truth we are guided by two sen-
tences, which we read in a study concerning the fascist
politician:

> *He hails from an ancient family from Gömör, [...] He had
> a sister Margit and a brother Sándor Hubay (born 14
> February 1898). Sándor has written literary articles, like
> his younger brother, and even wrote mathematical and
> physics-related papers. He worked as volunteer for the city
> meteorological station, he was an excellent student who
> exerted himself fully even in the musical choir...*

Source: Attila Godzsák: Hubay Kálmán ifjúkora és miskolci
újságírói pályája *[Kálmán Hubay, his youth and career as a journalist in Miskolc].* Széphalom 25. Yearbook of the Ferenc
Kazinczy Society, *2015.*

It is very likely that the same Dr. Sándor Hubay features as a
person welcoming, according to a contemporary newsreel,
Count Mihály Teleki, the Minister for Agriculture at the
Exhibition of the Export Office in 1939. He was among the illus-
trious participants, amongst numerous scientists, featured in
the representative brochure of this important public event:
"The life story of our Hungarian nation" (Lectures by Count Pál
Teleki, Bálint Hóman, Lajos Bartucz, Antal Klemm, Mihály
Kerék, Ödön Lukács, Béla Johan, Sándor Hubay, Tibor Gyulay,
Zoltán Koós, Károly Kresz, Gyula Bisztray, Iván Kotsis, Jenő

Kopp, Aladár Richter, Lajos Bárdos, János Hankiss). Fehérvári iskolahét, 1938. Edited by Brunó Balassa (Székesfehérvár, 1939). The detailed index of contents features a lecture by Sándor Hubay, entitled: "Hungarian agriculture." So far everything fits together and seems fairly predictable. But what follows—even if not incredible—is certainly surprising at the first glance. The Yad Vashem Memorial, etched in stone, also lists as rescuers during the Shoah the names of Sándor Hubay and his wife Katalin Nádosy. According to the account, a woman escaped from the ghetto, and with false Aryan papers reported to an employment office, seeking a job as a housemaid. The wife of the high-ranking military officer, who hailed from an "ancient aristocratic family," chose this lady and employed her as a live-in housekeeper. When the truth emerged, the family bravely undertook to hide her, and treated the boy as their own. After the Arrow Cross coup, the military officer sent away the brigands raiding the houses for hidden Jews, with the comment: "There have never been Jews here, and he, as a high-ranking officer would not have tolerated any such around him." All this was attested by Peter Klein who grew up in Israel and came back to Hungary for a visit 40 years later. That this is the same Sándor Hubay mentioned in the diary sounds so romantic that we could seriously become suspicious. However, not only does the name match in the two historical sources cited above, but the birth date is identical. So, either one of the two documents took the details from the other, or the two are independent, and the story is true. Why should it not be?

16 **Saturday afternoon we went to Tahi**: a fairly enigmatic entry. The use of plural suggests a group excursion of some sort. Sleeping in Tahi corresponds closely with some information as shown below: "The social service provided by the Budapest Christian Youth Association has an important highlight, which is an excursion by boat, usually to Tahi, to the conference cen-

tre of the high school students." (Bálint Kovács: *A Keresztyén Ifjúsági Egyesület története 1883–1950* [The history of the Christian Youth Society 1883–1950]. Budapest, 1998). Clearly László had links with the Protestant student communities, but how exactly—as a "Jewish tourist"—he experienced the hostile sentiments exhibited by the people of Visegrád is unclear from this report.

17 **BszKRT**: Budapest Transport Directorate.

18 **Béla Imrédy** (1891–1946): key politician of the interwar years, playing a crucial role in the pro-Nazi orientation of the country. Before entering politics, he was a renowned technocrat, expert in the field of monetary politics, serving as minister of finances and president of the National Bank. In 1938, the growing pressure from the extreme right pushed governor Miklós Horthy and prime minister Kálmán Darányi to invite this experienced economic expert to create a governmental program that both fulfilled some of the demands of the extreme right in implementing anti-Semitic policies, but still preserved the capitalist framework of the national economy. Thus, he was playing a key role in formulating the first anti-Jewish law and the Győr Program, announcing a massive state investment in developing military industry which was also meant to revitalize the economy. When it became clear that these measures did not stop the expansion of the extreme right but in some ways even reinforced it, Imrédy started to move towards fascism, also getting increasingly fascinated by the personality cult around Mussolini and Hitler. He envisioned a totalitarian power concentration coupled with a generous social program to be financed mainly from the confiscated Jewish property. He also sought to cooperate with Hitler in the destruction of Czechoslovakia. Imrédy offered his support in exchange for the German help in satisfying Hungary's territorial demands. After the successful re-con-

quest of territories in Upper Hungary, Imrédy considered his position strong enough to expand his power, limiting parliamentary control and also in some ways challenging the position of Horthy. Losing the support of the governor and of the more mainstream conservative faction of the government party, he radicalized further and tried to organize a fascist mass-party, but he was eventually forced to resign. It was an irony of destiny that his resignation was triggered by a document proving that one of his great-grandmothers was Jewish. After he resigned, he continued to aspire for the position of a fascist dictator but eventually Hitler opted for the Arrow Cross movement and Szálasi after the failure of Horthy's attempt to break with the Axis in October 1944.

19 **The first "anti-Jewish Law"**: in April 1938 the Darányi Government proposed a statute with the euphemistic title, "Regulating more effectively the balance in social and economic conditions." It aimed at restricting the proportion of Jews in the liberal professions, and limit their employment by financial, commercial, and industrial firms. The proposal began to be debated in parliament on 5 May 1938 and voted into law on 29 May 1938 by the Imrédy Government. Fifty-nine notable intellectuals and public personalites (including the above-mentioned Géza Féja, as well as artists Béla Bartók, Zoltán Kodály, and Zsigmond Móricz), signed a protest against the legal edict which stripped citizens of their legal rights.

20 **László Ravasz** (1882–1975): born in Transylvania, from 1921 elected as bishop, he was a leading Calvinist clergyman in interwar Hungary. His political position was conservative, equally critical of liberalism, socialism, and the extreme right. He supported the anti-Semitic legislation in the late 1930s, but in 1944 he took an active stance against the deportations.

21 **Immanuel Löw** (1854–1944): rabbi of Szeged and a prominent Jewish scholar. His father was also a leading figure of Hungarian Neolog (Reform) Judaism. He worked in the fields of Hebraic linguistics and Talmudic scholarship. From 1927, he represented the Neolog Jewish community in the Upper House of the Hungarian Parliament. In 1944, at the age of 90, he was deported to Auschwitz, but due to the intervention of leading Hungarian clergymen he was released from the train in Budapest. He died there a month later.

22 **Béla Paulini** (1881–1945): journalist and graphic designer. As a co-author, in 1926, he wrote the lyrics of Zoltán Kodály's successful musical play, *János Háry*, together with Zsolt Harsányi. In 1931 he started the movement of folk art, entited "Gyöngyösbokréta" (wreath of pearls), which sought to uncover local folkloric treasures. By setting these on the stage he intended to strengthen the peasantry's national and social identity. The relation of these performances to authentic peasant culture was highly debatable.

23 **Felvidék**: Upper-Hungary, present-day Slovakia; the territories lost to Czechoslovakia after WWI.

24 **Deanna Durbin**: popular Canadian film star; at that time she had up to four films showing in Budapest. *Nightingale of Hearts* was a joyful story about a great star and her daughter, who finds a husband for her mother.

25 **Imre Groszman** (?): clearly an important personality in László's life, because his emigration-related initiatives are tied up with him. We found such a name on the internet with minimal biographical detail (born in Mezőnagyszentmihály in 1912 – died in Russia as forced laborer). Although thought-provoking, we have no data or knowledge of his activities to compare to the

references in the Diary. It may be that there was a different individual, a Zionist, who may have survived the Shoah. (Similarly, we have been unable to identify the key players in the discussions associated with emigration, whether hosts or lawyers.) As far as the wartime Jewish rescue organizations are concerned – their review exceeds the framework of this volume.

26 **Eszter Waldapfel** (1906–1968): László's sister. She gained her degree at Péter Pázmány University of Budapest. She also attended the University of Vienna as a member of the Collegium Hungaricum, enrolled in legal history, and conducted research at the *Staatsarchiv* (1930–31). She worked later as a librarian. While his older brothers were all married with children, the bachelor László lived with his unmarried sister in a shared apartment throughout the 1930s.

27 **The Goldmark Hall**: housed by the Pest Jewish religious community headquarters behind the Synagogue in Dohány Street. It provided a venue for performances of banned Jewish artists between 1939 and 1944.

28 **Frigyes Décsi** (born Frigyes Docskál, 1912–1978): he studied and completed his degree at the Péter Pázmány University between 1929 and 1934 as a mathematics and physics teacher. He changed his name from Docskál to the more Hungarian-sounding Décsi. After military service he worked at the pedagogic faculty of the University, later in the Pension Institute of the Price Control Association. From 1937, he was employed by the State Meteorological Institute. On 15 April 1939, he reported to the Royal Hungarian Air Force official staff. He performed service at Mátyásföld and Budaörs in the capacity of time signaler.

Source: Antal Simon: Magyarországi meteorológusok életrajzi lexikonja *[The Biographical Encyclopaedia of Hungarian Meteorologists], website of the Hungarian Meteorological Society:* www.met.hu

29 **Pál (Paul) Erdős** (1913–1996): he was an extremely versatile and globally influential mathematician, working in the fields of discrete mathematics, graph theory, number theory, mathematical analysis, set theory, and probability theory. In 1938 he got a scholarship to Princeton and lived through the war years in the USA.

30 **Tibor Gallai** (born Tibor Grünwald, 1912–1992): he was a prominent mathematician, who worked in combinatorics, especially in graph theory.

31 In the original **behóved**, a Hebraism meaning respectable, honorable.

32 **Vázsonyi-era**: Vilmos Vázsonyi (1868–1926) was a prominent liberal politician at the turn of the century and, for a short while, minister of justice in 1917. A symbol of the successful integration of Jews into Hungarian liberal society, his efforts came to be considered illusory from the perspective of the growth of anti-Jewish discrimination after 1919. Vázsonyi was a complex personality, of a Jewish background and remaining loyal to his Jewish identity while being a Hungarian national liberal politician. A hero of the Jewish petite bourgeoisie in Budapest, he was a committed fighter for the rights of Hungarian Jews, supporting cultural assimilation but preserving an element of specific Jewish identity. From the perspective of the Diary, he appears as an iconic person of the past, contrasted to the present of forced dissimilation and the reversion of emancipation. At the same time, we must not overlook the ambigu-

ous feelings evoked by the luxurious flat dating from a liberal and affluent era…

33 **Baron Alfonz Weiss** (1890–1992): son of the industrial magnate Manfréd Weiss, one of the most influential leaders of the largest industrial conglomerate in Hungary.

34 **The Betar Group**: Betar was founded in Hungary in 1928, initially as a sports subdivision of the Zionist Organization of Hungary, and later in 1935 it became a separate organization. The Betar group was on the right wing of Zionism, emphasizing military tasks and preparedness.

This attitude would have evoked admiration and amazement in Jewish public life known for its urban, liberal sympathies. The attitude of Betar confronting the Jewish youth brought up by the Jewish public leadership was also critical. (…). The excoriation of assimilation in Hungary had few such virulent examples as Szilágyi (one of the founders of Betar), expressed in his selected works, entitled 'Education for a National Revolution'. (…) Even more interesting is the part entitled 'We and the Hungarians,' which points out the dissimilation from the majority, as the only possible route to follow, according to the author …If you love someone, but they do not love you in return, then – if you are healthy and sensitive enough close your heart to your love. You may perish, but do not run after a cart from which they toss you out with cruel curses. 'Do you really feel, brother, whose native tongue is Hungarian that you must live and die here?'. 'Grit your teeth, do not humiliate yourself, there exists no patriotism which demands that the patriot be spineless.' He addressed those who regarded patriotism as their 'civic duty,' in spite of discrimination, saying: 'It is not your civic duty to work against the will of the Hungarians, for their benefit. The Hungarians know better what they need than you do. Do not force your labor onto them, even though you may regard it as beneficial. We Zionists know that there are no liberating roads, here in Hungary. Roads leading to liberty only exist in one place. The Jewish state, in Palestine.' Szilágyi put his latter thesis into practice, as a co-organizer of one the last, large-scale, illegal aliya actions in a Europe about to plunge into war.

Source: *Bernát László Veszprémi:* Egy „holtig betári" – Szilágyi Dénes radikális cionista munkássága *["Betar to the grave" – Dénes Szilágyi's radical Zionist activities], in:* Múlt és Jövő 79 (2018) No 2–3.

35 **Returning from Révfülöp**: the expression suggests that compared to his excursion to Badacsony, Révfülöp has been a relatively more relaxing resting place for László in August 1940. A more precise delineation of circumstances would be of great help in the unravelling of the network of this young man, who mostly speaks in the first-person plural. In connection with this, however, the Diary offers no help whatsoever.

We might get some additional information from two post-cards sent to his older brother. Two of them were sent form Révfülöp. One is dated exactly one day after this entry concerning Révfülöp, to June 1939, while the other is dated 8 August. The text is not very interesting but in the free space two women's signatures are visible – one is *Kata,* the other is *Magda Kakassy.* Magda is possibly identical with the "child," who on 3 October 1935 as a 15-year-old girl, argued in a rather silly manner with the men in the corridors of the factory office who were about to assess the chances of a world war arising out of the Italian-Abyssinian conflict. In light of this, László could have visited Révfülöp repeatedly as a member of a workplace-based group. But we could not get much further along this path.

36 **"A Kiss and Nothing Else"**: the title of a popular operetta by Mihály Eisemann.

37 **Miklós Radnóti** (1909–1944): one of the most important Hungarian poets of the 20th century. Started his university studies in 1930 in Szeged and received his diploma in Hungarian and French literature and pedagogy. In 1936 he got a teaching qualification but could not get a teaching job because of his Jewish origins. In the university he was influenced by the Art College of Szeged Youth (Szegedi Fiatalok Művészeti Kollégiuma), an association of students aiming at reform in arts, culture, and social politics. He was also shaped by his spiritual mentor, Sándor Sík (1889–1963). Sík was a Piarist teacher, poet, literary historian, and boy scout leader (also of Jewish origin), who organized special literary seminars for his students. Radnóti converted to Catholicism in 1943 under the influence of Sík. His motivation can be discerned from his Diary (published in 1989), namely from a letter to the Zionist literary scholar Aladár Komlós, which he also copied into his diary, turning down an invitation to participate in an anthology of Jewish poets. (While the letter was written before his formal conversion, his identity was most probably the same as a year later.):

> *(...) I never reneged my Jewishness and I am even now belonging to the Jewish denomination (I will explain later, why), but I do not feel Jewish, I was never taught to be religious, I do not feel a need for it, I don't practice it. Race, blood ties, inseverable roots, ancient pangs quivering in every fiber—I consider such things utter nonsense, and not the defining characteristic of either my intellectuality, my spirituality, or my poetry. Even in the social sense I see the "community of Jews" as a bogus designation. This has been my experience. Perhaps it isn't so, but this is how I feel, and I could never live a lie. My Jewishness has become the prob-*

lem of my life, but it is circumstances, laws, the world that made it so. The problem was forced on me. Otherwise I am a Hungarian poet (...) I feel the same today, in 1942, after three months of labor service and fourteen days of punishment camp (...) forced out of literature, where petty poets who do not reach up to my heals are running up and down, with my useless and unused teacher's certificate in my pocket, and in full knowledge of the days, months, and years to come. And if they kill me? It will not change this either. (...)

(...) if I have anything to do with any religion it is with Catholicism. At the very beginning of my career as a poet, at the age of twenty-two, my second volume was confiscated and I was put on trial because of blasphemy. (...) it almost cost my place at the university. I was saved by Sándor Sík, what is more, in the name of the Piarist order he issued a letter for the court hearing, stating that from the perspective of the Church there was nothing questionable in the poem. The Court eventually suspended the punishment, and since then it expired. It was then that I decided to convert, not to employ the symbols of the "other religion," because for me this is not "another religion," the poetry of the Gospels belongs to me as much as that of the Old Testament and I also "believe" in Jesus, I do not find a better word, even though belief is ... but as it got worse and worse to be a Jew, here and there I could have profited from changing my religion, so it distorted it; (...) Eventually I stayed with the Jewish denomination. But from the perspective of my poetic self this is unimportant."

We drew on the translation by *Ivan Sanders, "Jewish Themes and Issues in Post-1989 Hungarian Literature,"* Hungarian Studies 18, No. 2 (2005): 213–222.

Indeed, Radnóti did not profit from his conversion. In 1944 he was again mobilized to work service and never returned home, being shot on the forced march toward the Austrian border.

Seemingly, we have given a bit too much space to Miklós Radnóti in this volume focusing on the diary of László Waldapfel. But we trust that the reader will understand why. We do not have evidence as to whether the poet knew personally his contemporary whose life ended in a similar way to his, or only his two elder brothers (Imre and József), to whom he addressed the letter we included in the appendix, expressing his sympathies after László's tragic death. But the most important analogy between the two is obviously not the similarity of the end of their lives, rather the converging patterns of their generational experience and search for identity.

38 **Counting of Omer**: a Jewish ritual, counting the 49 days that separate Passover and Shavuot.

39 **János Waldapfel** (1866–1935): born at Nagy-Zablát (*Slo.* Veľké Záblatie). Matriculated in 1882 at the Catholic High School in Trencsén; between 1882 and 1887 studied at the University of Budapest. From 1887 he translated articles from English for *Magyar Föld*, an economy journal. In 1894 he was a guest student at the University of Jena. After obtaining his doctorate in 1896, he was appointed to the Budapest Teachers' Training High School, teaching pedagogy and German language. He carried out his pedagogic work in the spirit of the "national liberalism" of the nineteenth century, in the environment marked by his mentor, Mór Kármán, himself of Jewish

origin, who carried on the reformist liberal traditions of József Eötvös. After 1919, with the demise of liberalism and the growth of anti-Semitism, he was marginalized and in 1924 he was pensioned.

It is thought-provoking that from 1935 only two entries are noted in the Diary. One of them dates from the end of May, the day of starting a job; the second entry was written on 3 October, two days before his father's passing. Subsequent to this, for two and a half years there is a pause. Thus, there is not a word about the death of his father. Neither is there any comment about other family-related events, although all three brothers have extended their families with children born in this period.

"Dad"

40 **Imre Trencsényi-Waldapfel** (1908–1970): classical philologist, historian of literature and comparative religious studies. He graduated in 1932 from Péter Pázmány University, belonging to the circle of students around Károly Kerényi (with the translator of Homer Gábor Devecseri, the folklorist János Honti, the Egyptologist Aladár Dobrovits, the historian of religion Angelo Brelich, and the art historian, János György Szilágyi). He earned a living until 1938 with occasional publications and editorial work. The focus of his scientific contributions was Greek mythology and the literature of Humanism. During the war he was repeatedly drafted to labor service. On 15 October 1944, the day of the Arrow Cross coup, he escaped and established contact with social democratic and communist resistance groups. In 1945 he took part in the reorganization of cultural life of Budapest and became a protagonist of a new left-wing child movement (the pioneer movement), which—with the establishment of the communist mono-party system—eventually became hegemonic. In 1948 he became university professor and in 1949 Rector of Szeged University, after which he moved back to Budapest, also serving as a Rector. After 1953 he was working as head of the Classical Philology Department. In 1956–1957, vocally supporting the regime, he again held political functions, among others in the reorganization of the pioneer movement. After the early 1960s he was able to focus more on his scholarly interests and published a number of important works and translations from ancient Greek and Latin.

41 **József Waldapfel** (1904–1968): László's older brother, in age betwen Gábor and Imre. He graduated at the Péter Pázmány University in 1925. He taught at the National Rabbinical Seminar afterwards. He was a literary historian, focusing on Hungarian enlightenment and romantic literary culture. The pivotal focus of his interest was *Bán Bánk* by József Katona, an early 19th century drama, which he reinterpreted and turned into a central

piece of the literary canon. In the 1950s he also held important positions but after 1956 he was less prominent in the emerging Kádárist cultural politics. In the 1960s, his interest in national romanticism became an inspiration for a younger generation of literary historians seeking to rehabilitate the intellectual traditions of "national liberalism."

42 **János Pruzsinszky** (1862–?): A teacher at the Ágoston Trefort Secondary Grammar School. He worked there at almost the same time as László's father, János Waldapfel, teaching Latin and Greek.